Be Transformed

New Testament
BE Books
by Warren Wiersbe

Be Loyal *(Matthew)*
Be Diligent *(Mark)*
Be Compassionate *(Luke 1–13)*
Be Courageous *(Luke 14–24)*
Be Alive *(John 1–12)*
Be Transformed *(John 13–21)*
Be Dynamic *(Acts 1–12)*
De Daring *(Acts 13–28)*
Be Right *(Romans)*
Be Wise *(1 Corinthians)*
Be Encouraged *(2 Corinthians)*
Be Free *(Galatians)*
Be Rich *(Ephesians)*
Be Joyful *(Philippians)*
Be Complete *(Colossians)*
Be Ready *(1 & 2 Thessalonians)*
Be Faithful *(1 & 2 Timothy, Titus, Philemon)*
Be Confident *(Hebrews)*
Be Mature *(James)*
Be Hopeful *(1 Peter)*
Be Alert *(2 Peter, 2 & 3 John, Jude)*
Be Real *(1 John)*
Be Victorious *(Revelation)*

Be
Transformed

AN EXPOSITORY OF JOHN 13-21

Warren W.
Wiersbe

David C Cook®
transforming lives together

BE TRANSFORMED
Published by David C. Cook
4050 Lee Vance View
Colorado Springs, CO 80918 U.S.A.

David C. Cook Distribution Canada
55 Woodslee Avenue, Paris, Ontario, Canada N3L 3E5

David C. Cook U.K., Kingsway Communications
Eastbourne, East Sussex BN23 6NT, England

David C. Cook and the graphic circle C logo
are registered trademarks of Cook Communications Ministries.

Most Scripture quotations are from the King James Version of the Bible. (Public
Domain.) Other quotations are from the *The New American Standard Bible*
(NASB), © the Lockman Foundation 1960, 1977; *The New Testament in Modern
English* (PH), Revised Edition, © J.B. Phillips, 1958, 1960, 1972, permission of
Macmillan Publishing Co. and Collins Publishing House.

LCCN 86-60874
ISBN 978-0-89693-352-1

©1986 Cook Communications Ministries

Cover Design: iDesignEtc.
Cover Photo: ©PhotoDisc Inc.
Study Questions: Lin Johnson

Printed in the United States of America
First Edition 1986

27 28 29 30 31 32 33 34 35 36

020808

CONTENTS

This book is for
Bob and Gertrude Spradling

*special friends who are
a lot of fun to know*

PREFACE

This book is a companion volume to *Be Alive!* a study of John 1–12.

The basic theme of John's Gospel is that Jesus Christ of Nazareth is the very Son of God, and all who believe on Him receive eternal life (20:30-31). John's *subject* is the deity of Christ. John's *object* is to lead people into the life—eternal life, abundant life—that only Christ can give. John is both a theologian and an evangelist.

The first twelve chapters focus on our Lord's public ministry, especially the signs (miracles) that Jesus performed and the messages that grew out of some of them. As you can see from the suggested outline, the climax of His public ministry was official rejection by the religious rulers of Israel.

In chapters 13–21, John presents, for the most part, the private ministry of Christ with His own disciples. He was preparing them for their future service when the Holy Spirit would come and empower them. It seems to me that what the disciples experienced during those days completely transformed their lives; hence, the title of this book—*Be Transformed.*

If you have not yet studied John 1–12, I suggest that you review those chapters with the outline before you so that you get acquainted with the development of the book.

WARREN W. WIERSBE

A Suggested Outline of John's Gospel

Key theme: Jesus is the Christ; believe and live!
Key verse: John 20:31

Prologue—1:1–14

I. OPPORTUNITY (1:15—6:71)
"Mine hour is not yet come" (2:4).
He presents Himself to:
1. His disciples, 1:19—2:12
2. The Jews, 2:13—3:36
3. The Samaritans, 4:1-54
4. The Jewish leaders, 5:1-47
5. The multitudes, 6:1-71.
Crisis 1—They would not walk with Him (6:66–71).

II. OPPOSITION (7:1—12:50)
"His hour was not yet come" (7:30).
There is conflict with the Jewish leaders over:
1. Moses, 7:1—8:11
2. Abraham, 8:12–59
3. Who Messiah is, 9:1—10:42
4. His miraculous power, 11:1–12:36.
Crisis 2—They would not believe on Him (12:37–50).

III. OUTCOME (13–21)
"His hour was come" (13:1; 17:1).
1. The faith of the disciples, 13–17
2. The unbelief of the Jews, 18–19
Crisis 3—They crucified Him (19:13–22).
                    The victory of Christ, 20—21

1

The Sovereign Servant

John 13:1-35

Three times in my ministry I have had to deliver "farewell messages" to congregations I had served, and it is not an easy thing to do. I may not have succeeded, but my purpose was always to prepare them for the future. This included warning as well as instruction. They would call a new pastor and enter into a new phase of ministry, and I wanted them to be at their best.

John 13–17 is our Lord's "farewell message" to His beloved disciples, climaxing with His intercessory prayer for them and for us. Other farewell addresses in Scripture were delivered by Moses (Deut. 31–33), Joshua (Josh. 23–24), and Paul (Acts 20). However, Jesus added a significant "action section" to His message when He washed His disciples' feet. It was an object lesson they would never forget.

In this passage, we see our Lord in a fourfold relationship: to His Heavenly Father (John 13:1-5), to Simon Peter (vv. 6-11), to all of the disciples (vv. 12-17), and to Judas (vv. 18-35). In each of these sections of John's Gospel, you will discover a special message, a spiritual truth to help you in your own Christian life.

1. Humility: Jesus and the Father (John 13:1-5)

Jesus had entered Jerusalem on Sunday, and on Monday had cleansed the temple. Tuesday was a day of conflict as the religious leaders sought to trip Him up and get evidence to arrest Him. These events are recorded in Matthew 21–25. Wednesday was probably a day of rest, but on Thursday He met in the Upper Room with His disciples in order to observe Passover.

The emphasis in vv. 1-3 is on *what our Lord knew*, and in vv. 4-5 on *what our Lord did.*

Jesus knew that "His hour was come." More than any of the Gospel writers, John emphasized the fact that Jesus lived on a "heavenly timetable" as He did the Father's will. Note the development of this theme:

2:4—"Mine hour is not yet come."

7:30—"His hour was not yet come."

8:20—"His hour was not yet come."

12:23—"The hour is come that the Son of man should be glorified."

13:1—"Jesus knew that His hour was come."

17:1—"Father, the hour is come."

What was this divinely appointed "hour"? It was the time when He would be glorified through His death, resurrection, and ascension. From the human point of view, it meant suffering; but from the divine point of view, it meant glory. He would soon leave this world and return to the Father, who sent Him, Jesus having finished His work on earth (17:4). When the servant of God is in the will of God, he is immortal until his work is done. They could not even arrest Jesus, let alone kill Him, until the right hour had arrived.

Jesus also knew that Judas would betray Him. Judas is mentioned eight times in John's Gospel, more than in any of the other Gospels. Satan had entered into Judas (Luke 22:3), and now he would give him the necessary thought to bring about the arrest and crucifixion of the Son of God. The word translated "put" in John 13:2 literally means "to throw." It reminds us of the fiery darts of the wicked one (Eph. 6:16). Judas was an unbeliever (John 6:64-71), so he did not have a "shield of faith" to use to ward off Satan's attacks.

Finally, Jesus knew that the Father had given Him all things (13:3). This statement parallels John 3:35, and it also reminds us of Matthew 11:27. Even in His humiliation, our Lord had all things through His Father. He was poor and yet He was rich. Because Jesus knew who He was, where He came from, what He had, and where He was going, He was complete master of the situation. You and I as believers know that we have been born of God, that we are one day going to God, and that in Christ we have all things; therefore, we ought to be able to follow our Lord's example and serve others.

What Jesus knew helped determine *what Jesus did* (John 13:4-5). The disciples must have been shocked when they saw their Master rise from supper, lay aside His outer garments, wrap a towel around His waist, take a basin of water and wash their feet. Jewish servants did not wash their masters' feet, although Gentile slaves might do it. It was a menial task, and yet Jesus did it! As a special mark of affection, a host or hostess might wash a guest's feet, but it was not standard operating procedure in most homes.

Jesus knew that there was a competitive spirit in the hearts of His disciples. In fact, within a few minutes, the men were disputing over which of them was the greatest (Luke 22:24-30)! He gave them an unforgettable lesson in humility, and by His actions rebuked their selfishness and pride. The more you think about this scene, the more profound it becomes. It is certainly an illustration of what Paul wrote years later in Philippians 2:1-16. Peter must have recalled the event when he wrote his first epistle and urged his readers to "be clothed with humility" (1 Peter 5:5).

Too often we confuse "the poor in spirit" (Matt. 5:3) with the "poor-spirited" and true humility with timidity and inferiority. The British literary giant Samuel Johnson was once asked to prepare a funeral sermon for a girl who had died, and he asked what her special virtues were. He was told that she was kind to her inferiors. Johnson replied that this was commendable, but that it would be difficult to determine who her inferiors were!

The Father had put all things into the Son's hands, *yet Jesus picked up a towel and a basin!* His humility was not born of poverty, but of riches. He was rich, yet He became poor (2 Cor. 8:9). A Malay proverb says, "The fuller the ear is of rice-grain, the lower it bends."

It is remarkable how the Gospel of John reveals the humility of our Lord even while magnifying His deity: "The Son can do nothing of Himself" (5:19, 30)./"For I came down from heaven, not to do Mine own will" (6:38)./"My doctrine is not Mine" (7:16)./"And I seek not Mine own glory" (8:50)./"The word which ye hear is not Mine" (14:24). His ultimate expression of humility was His death on the cross.

Jesus was the Sovereign, yet He took the place of a servant. He had all things in His hands, yet He picked up a towel. He was Lord and Master, yet He served His followers. It has well been said that humility is not thinking meanly of yourself; it is simply not thinking of yourself at all. True humility grows out of our relationship with the Father. If our desire is to know and do the Father's will so that we might glorify His name, then we will experience the joy of following Christ's example and serving others.

We today, just like the disciples that night, desperately need this lesson on humility. The church is filled with a worldly spirit of competition and criticism as believers vie with one another to see who is the greatest. We are growing in knowledge, but not in grace (see 2 Peter 3:18). "Humility is the only soil in which the graces root," wrote Andrew Murray. "The lack of humility is the sufficient explanation of every defect and failure."

Jesus served His disciples because of His humility and because of His love. Contrast John 13:1 with 1:11 and 3:16: Jesus came "unto His own [world], and His own [people] received him not."/"For God so loved the world." In the Upper Room, Jesus ministered in love to His own disciples, and they received Him and what He had to say. The Greek text says, "He loved them to the uttermost." And He still does!

2. Holiness: Jesus and Peter (John 13:6-11)

As Peter watched the Lord wash his friends' feet, he became more and more disturbed and could not understand what He was doing. As you read the life of Christ in the Gospels, you cannot help but notice how Peter often spoke impulsively out of his ignorance and had to be corrected by Jesus. Peter opposed Jesus going to the cross (Matt. 16:21-23), and he tried to manage our Lord's affairs at the Transfiguration (Matt. 17:1-8). He expressed the faith of the disciples (John 6:66-71) without realizing that one of the number was a traitor.

The word translated *wash* in verses 5, 6, 8, 12, and 14, is *niptō* and means "to wash a part of the body." But the word translated "washed" in verse 10 is *louō* and means "to bathe all over." The distinction is important, for Jesus was trying to teach His disciples the importance of a holy walk.

When the sinner trusts the Saviour, he is "bathed all over" and his sins are washed away and forgiven (see 1 Cor. 6:9-11; Titus 3:3-7; and Rev. 1:5). "And their sins and iniquities will I remember no more" (Heb. 10:17). However, as the believer walks in this world, it is easy to become defiled. He does not need to be bathed all over again; he simply needs to have that defilement cleansed away. God promises to cleanse us when we confess our sins to Him (1 John 1:9).

But why is it so important that we "keep our feet clean"? Because if we are defiled, we cannot have communion with our Lord. "If I wash thee not, thou hast no part with Me" (John 13:8). The word translated "part" is *meros*, and it carries the meaning here of "participation, having a share in someone or something." When God "bathes us all over" in salvation, He brings about our *union* with Christ; and that is a settled relationship that cannot change. (The verb *wash* in v. 10 is in the perfect tense. It is settled once and for all.) However, our *communion* with Christ depends on our keeping ourselves "unspotted from the world" (James 1:27). If we permit unconfessed sin in our lives, we hinder our walk with the Lord; and that is when we need to have our feet washed.

This basic truth of Christian living is beautifully illustrated in the Old Testament priesthood. When the priest was consecrated, he was bathed all over (Ex. 29:4), and that experience was never repeated. However, during his daily ministry, he became defiled; so it was necessary that he wash his hands and feet at the brass laver in the courtyard (Ex. 30:18-21). Only then could he enter the holy place and trim the lamps, eat the holy bread, or burn the incense.

The Lord cleanses us through the blood of Christ, that is, His work on the cross (1 John 1:5-10), and through the application of His Word to our lives (John 15:3; Eph. 5:25-26; Ps. 119:9). The "water of the Word" can keep our hearts and minds clean so that we will avoid the pollutions of this world. But if we do sin, we have a loving Advocate in glory who will hear our prayers of confession and forgive us (1 John 2:1-2).

Peter did not understand what his Lord was doing; but instead of waiting for an explanation, he impulsively tried to tell the Lord what to do. There is a strong double negative in John 13:8. The Greek scholar Kenneth Wuest translated Peter's statement, "You shall by no means wash my feet, no, never" (WUEST). Peter really meant it! Then when he discovered that to refuse the Lord would mean to lose the Lord's fellowship, he went in the opposite direction and asked for a complete bath!

We can learn an important lesson from Peter: don't question the Lord's will or work, and don't try to change it. He knows what He is doing. Peter had a difficult time accepting Christ's ministry to him *because Peter was not yet ready to minister to the other disciples.* It takes humility and grace to serve others, but it also takes humility and grace to allow others to serve us. The beautiful thing about a submissive spirit is that it can both give and receive to the glory of God.

John was careful to point out that Peter and Judas were in a different relationship with Jesus. Yes, Jesus washed Judas' feet! But it did Judas no good because he had not been bathed all over. Some people teach that Judas was a saved man who sinned away his salvation, but that is not what Jesus said. Our Lord made it very clear that Judas had never been cleansed from his sins and was an unbeliever (6:64-71).

It is a wonderful thing to deepen your fellowship with the Lord. The important thing is to be honest with Him and with ourselves and keep our feet clean.

3. Happiness: Jesus and the Disciples (John 13:12-17)
Verse 17 is the key—"If ye know these things, happy are ye if ye do them." The sequence is important: humbleness, holiness, then happiness. Aristotle defined happiness as "good fortune joined to virtue . . . a life that is both agreeable and secure." That might do for a philosopher, but it will never do for a Christian believer! Happiness is the by-product of a life that is lived in the will of God. When we humbly serve others, walk in God's paths of holiness, and do what He tells us, then we will enjoy happiness.

Jesus asked the disciples if they understood what He had done, and it is not likely that they did. So, He explained it: He had given them a lesson in humble service, an example for them to follow. The world thinks that happiness is the result of others serving us, but real joy comes when we serve others in the name of Christ. The world is constantly pursuing happiness, but that is like chasing a shadow: it is always just beyond your reach.

Jesus was their Master (Teacher) and Lord, so He had every

right to command their service. Instead, He served them! He gave them an example of true Christian ministry. On more than one occasion during the previous three years, He had taught them lessons about humility and service; but now He had demonstrated the lesson to them. Perhaps the disciples remembered His lesson about the child (Matt. 18:1-6), or the rebuke He gave James and John when they asked for thrones (Matt. 20:20-28). Now it was all starting to fall into place.

The servant (slave) is not greater than his master; so, if the master becomes a slave, where does that put the slave? *On the same level as the master!* By becoming a servant, our Lord did not push us down: He lifted us up! He dignified sacrifice and service. You must keep in mind that the Romans had no use for humility, and the Greeks despised manual labor. Jesus combined these two when He washed the disciples' feet.

The world asks, "How many people work for you?" but the Lord asks, "For how many people do you work?" When I was ministering at a conference in Kenya, an African believer shared one of their proverbs with me: "The chief is servant of all." How true it is that we need leaders who will serve and servants who will lead. G.K. Chesterton said that a really great man is one who makes others feel great, and Jesus did this with His disciples *by teaching them to serve.*

However, it is not enough just to *know* this truth; we must put it into practice. James 1:22-27 makes it clear that the blessing comes in the *doing* of the Word, not the hearing. Wuest translates the last phrase in James 1:25, "This man shall be prospered spiritually in his doing." Even studying this section in John's Gospel can stir us emotionally or enlighten us intellectually; but it cannot bless us spiritually until we do what Jesus told us to do. This is the only way to lasting happiness.

Be sure to keep these lessons in their proper sequence: humbleness, holiness, happiness. Submit to the Father, keep your life clean, and serve others. This is God's formula for true spiritual joy.

4. Hypocrisy: Jesus and Judas (John 13:18-35)

A dark shadow now falls across the scene as Jesus deals with Judas, the traitor. It is important to note that Judas was not a true believer; he was a hypocrite. He had never believed in Jesus (6:64-71), he had not been bathed all over (13:10-11), and he had not been among the chosen ones whom the Father gave to the Son (13:18 and 17:12). How close a person can come to salvation and yet be lost forever! Judas was even the treasurer of the group (12:6) and was certainly held in high regard by his fellow disciples.

At that hour, Jesus had two great concerns: to fulfill the Word of God (13:18-30) and to magnify the glory of God (vv. 31-35).

The Scripture Jesus quoted was Psalm 41:9—"Yea, mine own familiar friend, in whom I trusted, which did eat of my bread, hath lifted up his heel against me." When David wrote the psalm, he was probably referring to his counselor Ahithophel, who turned traitor and joined Absalom's rebellion (see 2 Sam. 15–17). It is significant that both Judas and Ahithophel committed suicide by hanging themselves (2 Sam. 17:23 and Matt. 27:3-10 and Acts 1:18). However, Judas did not commit suicide in order to fulfill biblical prophecy, for that would make God the author of his sin. Judas was responsible for his own decisions, and those decisions fulfilled God's Word.

Jesus was concerned that Judas' treachery would not weaken His disciples' faith. This is why He related it to the Word of God: when the disciples saw all of this fulfilled, it would make their faith stronger (see John 8:28). Judas had been disloyal, but He expected them to be loyal to Him and His cause. After all, He was God the Son sent by God the Father. They were Christ's chosen representatives; to receive them would be the same as receiving the Father and the Son. What a privilege, to be ambassadors of the King!

The remarkable thing is that the others at the table with Jesus did not know that Judas was an unbeliever and a traitor. Up to the very hour of his treachery, Judas was protected by the Saviour whom he betrayed. Had Jesus openly revealed what He knew about Judas, it is likely that the men would have turned upon him. Remember what Peter did to Malchus when soldiers came to take Jesus!

From the very beginning, Jesus knew what Judas would do (6:64), but He did not compel him to do it. Judas was exposed to the same spiritual privileges as the other disciples, yet they did him no good. The same sun that melts the ice only hardens the clay. In spite of all that our Lord said about money, and all of His warning about covetousness, Judas continued to be a thief and steal from the treasury. In spite of all our Lord's warning about unbelief, Judas persisted in his rejection. *Jesus even washed Judas' feet!* Yet his hard heart did not yield.

Jesus had spoken before about a traitor (6:70), but the disciples did not take it to heart. Now when He spoke openly about it at the table, His disciples were perplexed.

Peter signaled to John, who was the closest to Jesus at the table, and asked him to find out who the traitor was. The Lord's reply to John was certainly not heard by all the men; in fact, they were carrying on discussions among themselves about who the traitor might be (Luke 22:23). When Jesus gave the bread to Judas, it was interpreted as an act of love and honor. In fact, Judas was seated at the place of honor, so our Lord's actions were seen in that light: He was bestowing a special honor on Judas. No wonder, after Judas left the room, the disciples got into an argument over who was the greatest (Luke 22:24-30)!

John was no doubt stunned by this revelation, but before he could say or do anything, Jesus had sent Judas on his way. Even though Satan had entered Judas, it was Jesus who was in charge. He lived on the timetable given to Him by the Father, and He wanted to fulfill what was written in the Word. Since Judas was the treasurer, it was logical for the disciples to conclude that he had been sent on a special mission by the Lord. Judas had hypocritically expressed an interest in the poor (John 12:4-6), so perhaps he was on an errand of mercy to help the poor.

Keep in mind that Judas knew what he was doing and that he did it deliberately. He had already met with the Jewish religious leaders and agreed to lead them to Jesus in such a way that there would not be any public disturbance (Luke 21:37–22:6). He heard Jesus say, "Woe unto that man by whom the Son of man is betrayed! It had been good for that man if he had not been born!" (Matt. 26:24) Yet, he persisted in his unbelief and treachery.

John's little phrase "and it was night" carries a tremendous impact when you remember that *light* and *darkness* are important spiritual images in his Gospel. Jesus is the Light of the world (John 8:12), but Judas rejected Jesus and went out into darkness; and for Judas, *it is still night!* Those who do evil hate the light (3:18-21). Our Lord's warning in John 12:25-26 went unheeded by Judas—and it goes unheeded by lost sinners today, people who will go where Judas went unless they repent and trust the Saviour.

The instant Judas was gone, the atmosphere was cleared, and Jesus began to instruct His disciples and prepare them for His crucifixion and His ultimate return to heaven. It was after Judas' departure that He instituted the Lord's Supper, something that Judas as an unbeliever certainly could not share. Judas was out in the night, controlled by the prince of darkness, Satan; but Jesus was in the light, sharing love and truth with His beloved disciples. What a contrast!

The theme now changes to the glory of God (13:31-35). From the human perspective, the death of Christ was a dastardly deed involving unspeakable suffering and humiliation;

but from the divine perspective it was the revelation of the glory of God. "The hour is come that the Son of man should be glorified" (12:23). Twelve times in this Gospel, the title "Son of man" appears, and this one in verse 31 is the final instance. Daniel 7:13 identifies this title as messianic, and Jesus sometimes used it this way (Matt. 26:64).

What did it mean for Jesus to glorify the Father? He tells us in His prayer: "I have glorified Thee on the earth; I have finished the work which Thou gavest Me to do" (John 17:4). This is the way all of us glorify God, by faithfully doing what He calls us to do. In our Lord's case, the Father's will was that the Son die for lost sinners, be raised from the dead, and then ascend to heaven. The Son glorified the Father and the Father glorified the Son (17:1, 5).

There would come a time when the Son would be glorified in these disciples (17:10), but they could not follow Him at that time. Peter boasted that he would follow the Lord even to death (Luke 22:33), but unfortunately he followed and ended up denying Him three times.

Jesus had said to the Jews on two occasions that they would seek Him but not be able to find Him or follow Him (7:33-36; 8:21-24). Note that He did not tell His disciples that they would not be able to find Him, but He did say that to the unbelieving Jews. One day the believing disciples would go to be with Him (14:1-3), and they would also see Him after His resurrection. But during this time of His suffering and death, it was important that they not try to follow Him.

I have heard eloquent sermons about the sin of Peter who "followed afar off" (Luke 22:54), and the emphasis was that he should have followed nearer. The simple fact is that he should not have followed at all! The statement in verse 33 is proof enough, and when you add Matthew 26:31 (quoted from Zechariah 13:7) and our Lord's words in John 18:8, the evidence is conclusive. Because Peter disregarded this warning, he got into trouble.

The disciples' responsibility was to love one another just as Christ had loved them. They would certainly need this love in the hours to follow, when their Master would be taken from them and their brave spokesman, Peter, would fail Him and them. In fact, all of them would fail, and the only thing that would bring them together would be their love for Christ and for each other.

The word *love* is used only twelve times in John 1–12, but in chapters 13–21 it is used forty-four times! It is a key word in Christ's farewell sermon to His disciples, as well as a burden in His high priestly prayer (17:26). The word *new* does not mean "new in time," because love has been important to God's people even from Old Testament times (see Lev. 19:18). It means "new in experience, fresh." It is the opposite of "worn out." Love would take on a new meaning and power because of the death of Christ on the cross (15:13). With the coming of the Holy Spirit, love would have a new power in their lives.

This section begins and ends with love: Jesus' love for His own (v. 1) and the disciples' love for one another. It is love that is the true evidence that we belong to Jesus Christ. The church leader Tertullian (A.D. 155-220) quoted the pagans as saying of the Christians, "See how they love one another?" And how do we evidence that love? By doing what Jesus did: laying down our lives for the brethren (1 John 3:16). And the way to start is by getting down and washing one another's feet in sacrificial service.

2
Heart Trouble

John 13:36–14:31

This section opens and closes with our Lord's loving admonition, "Let not your heart be troubled" (14:1 and 27). We are not surprised that the apostles were troubled. After all, Jesus had announced that one of them was a traitor, and then He warned Peter that he was going to deny his Lord three times. Self-confident Peter was certain that he could not only follow his Lord, but even die with Him and for Him. Alas, Peter did not know his own heart, nor do we really know *our* hearts, except for one thing: our hearts easily become troubled.

Perhaps the heaviest blow of all was the realization that Jesus was going to leave them (13:33). Where was He going? Could they go with Him? How could they get where He was going? These were some of the perplexing questions that tumbled around in their minds and hearts and were tossed back and forth in their conversation at the table.

How did Jesus calm their troubled hearts? By giving them six wonderful assurances to lay hold of, assurances that we today may claim and thus enjoy untroubled hearts. If you are a believer in Jesus Christ, you may claim every single one of these assurances.

1. You Are Going to Heaven (John 13:36–14:6)

Jesus did not rebuke Peter for asking Him where He was going, but His reply was somewhat cryptic. One day Peter would "follow" Jesus to the cross (John 21:18-19; 2 Peter 1:12-15), and then he would follow Him to heaven. Tradition tells us that Peter was crucified, although he asked to be crucified head-downward because he did not feel worthy to die as his Master died.

Just as Peter was beginning to feel like a hero, Jesus announced that He Himself would soon become a casualty. The message not only shocked Peter, but it also stunned the rest of the disciples. After all, if brave Peter denies the Lord, what hope was there for the rest of them? It was then that Jesus gave His message to calm their troubled hearts.

According to Jesus, heaven is a real place. It is not a product of religious imagination or the result of a psyched-up mentality, looking for "pie in the sky by and by." Heaven is the place where God dwells and where Jesus sits today at the right hand of the Father. Heaven is described as a kingdom (2 Peter 1:11), an inheritance (1 Peter 1:4), a country (Heb. 11:16), a city (Heb. 11:16), and a home (John 14:2).

The word *Father* is used fifty-three times in John 13–17. Heaven is "My Father's house," according to the Son of God. It is "home" for God's children! Some years ago, a London newspaper held a contest to determine the best definition of "home." The winning entry was, "Home is the place where you are treated the best and complain the most." The poet Robert Frost said that home is the place that, when you arrive there, they have to take you in. A good definition!

The Greek word *monē* is translated "mansions" in verse 2 and "abode" in verse 23. It simply means "rooms, abiding places," so we must not think in terms of manor houses. It is unfortunate that some unbiblical songs have perpetuated the error that faithful Christians will have lovely mansions in glory, while worldly saints will have to be content with little cottages or even shacks. Jesus Christ is now preparing places for all true believers, and each place will be beautiful. When He was here on earth, Jesus was a carpenter (Mark 6:3). Now that He has returned to glory, He is building a church on earth and a home for that church in heaven.

John 14:3 is a clear promise of our Lord's return for His people. Some will go to heaven through the valley of the shadow of death, but those who are alive when Jesus returns will *never* see death (John 11:25-26). They will be changed to be like Christ and will go to heaven (1 Thes. 4:13-18).

Since heaven is the Father's house, it must be a place of love and joy. When the Apostle John tried to describe heaven, he almost ran out of symbols and comparisons (Rev. 21–22)! Finally, he listed the things that would not be there: death, sorrow, crying, pain, night, etc. What a wonderful home it will be—and we will enjoy it forever!

Thomas' question revealed his keen desire to be with Jesus (see John 11:16), and this meant that he had to know where the Master was going and how he himself would get there. The Lord made it clear that He was going to the Father, and that He was the only way to the Father. Heaven is a real place, a loving place, and an exclusive place. Not everybody is going to heaven, but rather only those who have trusted Jesus Christ (see Acts 4:12 and 1 Tim. 2:4-6).

Jesus does not simply teach the way or point the way; *He is the way*. In fact, "the Way" was one of the early names for the Christian faith (Acts 9:2; 19:9, 23; 22:4; 24:14, 22). Our Lord's statement "no man cometh unto the Father but by Me" wipes away any other proposed way to heaven—good works, religious ceremonies, costly gifts, etc. There is only one way, and that way is Jesus Christ.

How would this assurance of going to heaven help to calm the disciples' troubled hearts? Dr. James M. Gray put it beautifully in a song he wrote years ago: "Who could mind the journey, when the road leads home?" The assurance of a heavenly home at the end of life's road enables us to bear joyfully with the obstacles and battles along the way. It was this assurance that even encouraged our Lord, "who for the joy that was set before Him endured the cross" (Heb. 12:2). Paul had this truth in mind when he wrote, "For I reckon that the sufferings of this present time are not worthy to be compared with the glory which shall be revealed in us" (Rom. 8:18).

2. You Know the Father Right Now (John 14:7-11)

We do not have to wait until we enter heaven to get to know the Father. We can know Him today and receive from Him the spiritual resources we need to keep going when the days are difficult.

What does it mean to "know the Father"? The word *know* is used 141 times in John's Gospel, but it does not always carry the same meaning. In fact, there are four different "levels" of *knowing* according to John. The lowest level is simply knowing a fact. The next level is to understand the truth behind that fact. However, you can know the fact and know the truth behind it and still be lost in your sins. The third level introduces *relationship;* "to know" means "to believe in a person and become related to him or her." This is the way "know" is used in John 17:3. In fact, in Scripture, "to know" is used of the most intimate relationship between man and wife (Gen. 4:1).

The fourth use of "know" means "to have a deeper relationship with a person, a deeper communion." It was this level Paul was referring to when he wrote, "That I may know Him . . ." (Phil. 3:10). Jesus will describe this deeper relationship in John 14:19-23, so we will save any further comment until we deal with that section.

When Jesus said that knowing Him and seeing Him was the same as knowing and seeing the Father, He was claiming to be God. From now on, they would understand more and more about the Father, even though Jesus was leaving them.

I appreciate Philip's desire to know the Father. He had come

a long way since that day Jesus found him and called him
(1:43-45). The burning desire of every believer ought to be to
know God better. We read and study the Word of God so that
we might better know the God of the Word.

The Greek construction of the question in verse 10 indicates
that the Lord expected a yes answer from Philip: he *did* believe
that Jesus was in the Father and the Father in Him. That being
the case, Philip should have realized that the words of Jesus,
as well as His works, came from the Father and revealed the
Father. Believers today have not seen the Lord Jesus in the flesh
(1 Peter 1:8), but we do see Him and His works in the Word.
The emphasis throughout John's Gospel is that you cannot
separate Christ's words and works, for both come from the
Father and reveal the Father.

The "believe" in verse 10 is singular, for Jesus was address-
ing Philip; but in verse 11, it is plural and He addresses all of
the disciples. The tense of both is "go on believing." Let your
faith grow!

Four hundred years before Christ was born, the Greek
philosopher Plato wrote, "To find out the Father and Maker of
all this universe is a hard task, and when we have found Him,
to speak of Him to all men is impossible." But Plato was
wrong! We *can* know the Father and Maker of the universe, for
Jesus Christ revealed Him to us. Why should our hearts be
troubled when the Creator and Governor of the universe is *our
own Father?*

The very Lord of heaven and earth is our Father (Luke
10:21). There is no need for us to have troubled hearts, for He
is in control.

3. You Have the Privilege of Prayer (John 14:12-15)

"Why pray when you can worry?" asks a plaque that I have
seen in many homes. One of the best remedies for a troubled
heart is prayer.

"O what peace we often forfeit,
O what needless pain we bear;
All because we do not carry
Everything to God in prayer."

However, if God is going to answer our prayers and give us peace in our hearts, there are certain conditions that we must meet. In fact, the meeting of these conditions is a blessing in itself!

We must pray in faith (v. 12). This is a promise for us to claim, and the claiming of it demands faith. The double "verily" assures us that this is a solemn announcement. The fact that Jesus did return to the Father is an encouragement, for there He is interceding for us. He will have more to say about this intercessory work later in His discourse.

The "greater works [things]" would apply initially to the apostles who were given the power to perform special miracles as the credentials of their office (Heb. 2:3-4; Rom. 15:18-19). These miracles were not greater in *quality*, for "the servant is not greater than his lord" (13:16), but rather in scope and quantity. Peter preached one sermon and 3,000 sinners were converted in one day! The fact that ordinary people performed these signs made them even more wonderful and brought great glory to God (Acts 5:13-16).

Of course, it is not the believer himself who does these "greater things"; it is God working in and through the believer: "The Lord working with them" (Mark 16:20). "For it is God which worketh in you" (Phil. 2:13). Faith and works must always go together, for it is faith that releases the power of God in our lives.

We must pray in Christ's name (vv. 13-14). This is not a "magic formula" that we automatically attach to our prayer requests, guaranteeing that God will answer. To ask anything of the Father, in the name of Jesus, means that we ask what Jesus would ask, what would please Him, and what would bring Him glory by furthering His work. When a friend says to you, "You may use my name!" he is handing you a great privilege as well as a tremendous responsibility.

The "whatsoever" in verse 13 is qualified by all that God has revealed in His Word about prayer; likewise, the "anything" in verse 14. God is not giving us *carte blanche*; "in My name" is the controlling element. To know God's name means to know His nature, what He is, and what He wants to do. God answers prayer in order to honor His name; therefore, prayer must be in His will (1 John 5:14-15). The first request in "The Lord's Prayer" is, "Hallowed be Thy name" (Matt. 6:9). Any request that does not glorify God's name should not be asked in His name.

We must pray in loving obedience (v. 15). When you love someone, you honor his or her name; and you would never use that name in a demeaning manner. *Love* is an important theme in the Gospel of John; it is used as a verb or noun a total of fifty-six times.

Both love and obedience are part of effective prayer. "If I regard [see and approve] iniquity in my heart, the Lord will not hear me" (Ps. 66:18).

We do not obey the Lord simply because we want our prayers answered, somewhat like the attitude of a child just before Christmas. We obey Him because we love Him; and the more we obey Him, the more we experience His love. To "keep" His commandments means to value them, treasure them, guard them, and do them. "I have esteemed the words of His mouth more than my necessary food" (Job 23:12).

Believing prayer is wonderful medicine to soothe a troubled heart. Meditate on Philippians 4:6-7—and then put it into practice!

4. We Have the Holy Spirit (John 14:16-18)
Jesus had a great deal to say about the Holy Spirit in His Upper Room message, for apart from the help of the Spirit of God, we

cannot live the Christian life as God would have us live it. We must know who the Holy Spirit is, what He does, and how He does it.

The Holy Spirit is given two special names by our Lord: "another Comforter" and "the Spirit of truth." The Greek word translated "Comforter" is *paraklētos* and it is used only by John (14:16, 26; 15:26; 16:7; 1 John 2:1). It means "called alongside to assist." The Holy Spirit does not work instead of us, or in spite of us, but in us and through us.

Our English word *comfort* comes from two Latin words meaning "with strength." We usually think of "comfort" as soothing someone, consoling him or her; and to some extent this is true. But true comfort strengthens us to face life bravely and keep on going. It does not rob us of responsibility or make it easy for us to give up. Some translations call the Holy Spirit "the Encourager," and this is a good choice of words. *Paraklētos* is translated "Advocate" in 1 John 2:1. An "advocate" is one who represents you at court and stands at your side to plead your case.

As "the Spirit of truth," the Holy Spirit is related to Jesus, the Truth, and the Word of God, which of itself is the truth (John 14:6 and 17:17). The Spirit inspired the Word and also illumines the Word so we may understand it. Later on in this message, Jesus will explain the teaching ministry of the Holy Spirit. Since He is the "Spirit of truth," the Holy Spirit cannot lie or be associated with lies. He never leads us to do anything contrary to the Word of God, for again God's Word is truth.

If we want the Holy Spirit to work in our lives, we must seek to glorify Christ; and we must make much of the Word of God. When you compare Ephesians 5:18–6:9 with Colossians 3:16–4:1, you will see that both passages describe the same kind of Christian life—joyful, thankful, and submissive. To be filled with the Spirit is the same as to be controlled by the Word. The Spirit of truth uses the Word of truth to guide us into the will and the work of God.

The Holy Spirit abides in the believer. He is a gift from the Father in answer to the prayer of the Son. During His earthly ministry, Jesus had guided, guarded, and taught His disciples; but now He was going to leave them. The Spirit of God would come to them *and dwell in them*, taking the place of their Master. Jesus called the Spirit "another Comforter," and the Greek word translated "another" means "another of the same kind." The Spirit of God is not different from the Son of God, for both are God. The Spirit of God had dwelt *with* the disciples in the person of Jesus Christ. Now He would dwell *in* them.

Of course, the Spirit of God had been on earth before. He empowered men and women in the Old Testament to accomplish God's work. However, during the Old Testament age, the Spirit of God would come upon people and then leave them. God's Spirit departed from King Saul (1 Sam. 16:14 and 18:12); and David, when confessing his sin, asked that the Spirit not be taken from him (Ps. 51:11). When the Holy Spirit was given at Pentecost, He was given to God's people to remain with them forever. Even though we may grieve the Spirit, He will not leave us.

The way we treat the Holy Spirit is the way we treat the Lord Jesus Christ. The believer's body is the temple of the Spirit (1 Cor. 6:19-20), so what he or she does with that body affects the indwelling Holy Spirit. The Spirit wrote the Word of God, and the way we treat the Bible is the way we treat the Spirit of God and the Son of God.

The world cannot receive the Spirit because the world lives "by sight" and not by faith. Furthermore, the world does not know Jesus Christ; and you cannot have knowledge of the Spirit apart from the Son. The presence of the Spirit in this world is actually an indictment against the world, for the world rejected Jesus Christ.

The word translated "comfortless" in verse 18 means "orphans." We are not alone, abandoned, helpless and hopeless!

Wherever we go, the Spirit is with us, so why should we feel like orphans? There is no need to have a troubled heart when you have the very Spirit of God dwelling within you!

5. We Enjoy the Father's Love (John 14:19-24)

"The love of God is shed abroad in our hearts by the Holy Spirit which is given unto us" (Rom. 5:5). Orphans feel unwanted and unloved, but our Father shares His love with us. Jesus explained a threefold manifestation of God's love.

First, there was a *past manifestation to the disciples* (vv. 19-20). Verse 19 focuses on His resurrection and post-resurrection appearances to His disciples and other believers. The last time the world saw Jesus was when Joseph and Nicodemus took Him from the cross and buried Him. The next time the world sees Him, He will come in power and great glory to judge lost sinners.

Verse 20 centers especially on the coming of the Spirit at Pentecost and the oneness of the believers with their Lord. Jesus returned to heaven as the exalted Head of the church (Eph. 1:19-23); then He sent the Spirit so that the members of the body would be joined to their Head in a living union. Believers today, of course, did not see Jesus after His resurrection or in His ascension, but we are united to Him by the indwelling Holy Spirit.

There is a *present* manifestation of Himself to believers that you and I may enjoy today (vv. 21, 23-24). Note the repetition of the word *love*. If we treasure His Word and obey it, then the Father and the Son will share Their love with us and make Their home in us. The word translated "abode" in verse 23 means "make our home" and is related to "mansions" in verse 2.

When the sinner trusts Christ, he is born again and the Spirit immediately enters his body and bears witness that he is a child of God. The Spirit is resident and will not depart. But as the believer yields to the Father, loves the Word, prays, and obeys, there is a deeper relationship with the Father, Son, and Spirit. Salvation means we are going to heaven, but submission means that heaven comes to us!

This truth is illustrated in the experiences of Abraham and Lot, recorded in Genesis 18 and 19. When Jesus and the two angels visited Abraham's tent, they felt right at home. They even enjoyed a meal, and Jesus had a private talk wth Abraham. But our Lord did not go to Sodom to visit Lot, because He did not feel at home there. Instead, He sent the two angels.

Our experience with God ought to go deeper and deeper, and it will as we yield to the Spirit of truth and permit Him to teach us and guide us. If we love God and obey Him, He will manifest His love to us in a deeper way each day.

There will also be *a future manifestation* of God's love when Jesus Christ returns (v. 19). Judas (not Iscariot) recalled that Jesus had said He would not manifest Himself to the world (v. 22). But this seemed to contradict other statements He had made, such as recorded in Matthew 24:30. His question was, "What has come to pass that You are no longer going to reveal Yourself to the world?" Has there been a change in the divine plan?

Jesus had been rejected by His own people, so He could not manifest Himself to them. In fact, it was an act of mercy that He did not manifest Himself to the world, because that would have meant judgment. He has revealed Himself to His church and left the church in the world to be a witness of God's love. He is patiently waiting, still giving lost sinners opportunity to repent and be saved (2 Peter 3:1-10). One day He will return (Rev. 1:7) and the world will behold Him.

One of the best ways to ease a troubled heart is to bathe it in the love of God. When you feel like an "orphan," let the Spirit of God reveal God's love to you in a deeper way. Charles Spurgeon said, "Little faith will take your soul to heaven, but great faith will bring heaven to your soul." Your heart can become a "heaven on earth" as you commune with the Lord and worship Him.

6. You Have His Gift of Peace (John 14:25-31)

Shalom—peace—is a precious word to the Jewish people. It means much more than just the absence of war or distress. *Shalom* means wholeness, completeness, health, security, even prosperity in the best sense. When you are enjoying God's peace, there is joy and contentment. But God's peace is not like the "peace" that the world offers.

The world bases its peace on its *resources,* while God's peace depends on *relationships.* To be right with God means to enjoy the peace of God. The world depends on personal ability, but the Christian depends on spiritual adequacy in Christ. In the world, peace is something you hope for or work for; but to the Christian, peace is God's wonderful gift, received by faith. Unsaved people enjoy peace when there is an absence of trouble; Christians enjoy peace *in spite of trials* because of the presence of power, the Holy Spirit.

People in the world walk by sight and depend on the externals, but Christians walk by faith and depend on the eternals. The Spirit of God teaches us the Word and guides us (not drags us!) into the truth. He also reminds us of what He has taught us so that we can depend on God's Word in the difficult times of life. The Spirit uses the Word to give us His peace (14:27), His love (15:9-10), and His joy (15:11). If that does not calm a troubled heart, nothing will!

Again, Jesus assured them that they would see Him again (v. 28). Why rejoice because He returned to the Father? Because His return made possible His wonderful intercessory ministry on our behalf, our great High Priest in heaven (Heb. 2:17-18; 4:14-16). We have the Spirit within us, the Saviour above us, and the Word before us! What tremendous resources for peace!

In verses 30 and 31, the Lord named two of our great

spiritual enemies—the world and the devil. Jesus overcame the world and the devil (12:31), and the devil has no claim on Him. There is no point in Jesus Christ where the devil can get a foothold. Since we are "in Christ," Satan can get no foothold in the believer's life, unless we permit it. Neither Satan nor the world can trouble our hearts if we are yielded to the "peace of God" through the Holy Spirit.

When Jesus said "My Father is greater than I" (v. 28), He was not denying His own deity or His equality with God, for then He would have been contradicting Himself (10:30). When Jesus was here on earth, He was necessarily limited by having a human body. He voluntarily laid aside the independent exercise of His divine attributes and submitted Himself to the Father. In that sense, the Father was greater than the Son. Of course, when the Son returned to heaven, all He had laid aside was restored once again (17:1, 5).

Jesus showed His love for the Father (and for the world) by voluntarily going to the cross. He did not hide or flee. He willingly laid down His life. He and the disciples may have left the Upper Room at this point (v. 31) so that what Jesus said from that point on was spoken on the way to the garden. Or, they may have arisen from the table and lingered awhile as He instructed them. We can easily imagine the allegory of the vine being given as they walked that night through the vineyards.

His own perfect peace assures us that He alone can give true peace. Jesus was always the Master of the situation, and He enables us to take control of our lives as we surrender to Him and receive His legacy of peace.

3
Relationships and Responsibilities

John 15:1-17

This is the seventh and last of the "I AM" statements of Christ recorded in the Gospel of John. However, Jesus did not stop with this image, but went on to use the picture of "the friend." These two pictures of the believer—branches and friends— reveal both our privileges and our responsibilities. As *branches*, we have the privilege of sharing His life, and the responsibility of abiding. As *friends*, we have the privilege of knowing His will, and the responsibility of obeying.

1. Branches—We Must Abide (John 15:1-11)
The cultivation of vineyards was important to the life and economy of Israel. A golden vine adorned Herod's temple. When our Lord used this image, He was not introducing something new; it was familiar to every Jew. There are four elements in this allegory that we must understand if we are to benefit from His teaching.

(1) *The vine.* There are actually three different vines found in Scripture. The *past* vine was the nation of Israel. (See Psalm 80:8-19, Isaiah 5:1-7, Jeremiah 2:21, Ezekiel 19:10-14, and Hosea 10:1.) In an act of wonderful grace, God "transplanted"

Israel into Canaan and gave the nation every possible benefit. "What could have been done more to My vineyard, that I have not done in it?" God asked (Isa. 5:4). If ever a nation had everything it needed to succeed, it was Israel.

But the vine produced wild grapes! Instead of practicing justice, it practiced oppression; instead of producing righteousness, it produced unrighteousness and cries of distress from the victims. God had to deal with the nation Israel and chasten it, but even that did not produce lasting results. When God's own Son came to the vineyard, they cast Him out and killed Him (Matt. 21:33-46).

There is also a *future* vine, "the vine of the earth" described in Revelation 14:14-20. This is the Gentile world system ripening for God's judgment. Believers are branches in "the vine of heaven," but the unsaved are branches in "the vine of the earth." The unsaved depend on this world for their sustenance and satisfaction, while believers depend on Jesus Christ. The "vine of the earth" will be cut down and destroyed when Jesus Christ returns.

The *present* Vine is our Lord Jesus Christ, and, of course, the vine includes the branches. He is the "true Vine," that is, "the original of which all other vines are a copy." As Christians, we do not live on substitutes! The symbolism of the Vine and branches is similar to that of the Head and the body: we have a living relationship to Christ and belong to Him.

When we lived in Chicago, we had a small grape arbor in our backyard; but what we cultivated was nothing like what is even today cultivated in the Holy Land. Ours was a very fragile plant and it was easy to break off a branch. The vines I saw in the Holy Land were large and strong, and it was next to impossible for anyone to break off a mature branch *without injuring the vine itself.* Our union with Christ is a *living* union, so we may bear fruit; a *loving* union, so that we may enjoy Him; and a *lasting* union, so that we need not be afraid.

(2) *The branches.* Of itself, a branch is weak and useless. It

is good for either bearing or burning, but not for building. (Read Ezekiel 15.) The branch cannot produce its own life; it must draw that life from the vine. It is our communion with Christ through the Spirit that makes possible the bearing of the fruit.

Many of the images of Christ and the believer given in Scripture emphasize this important concept of *union and communion:* the body and its members (1 Cor. 12), the bride and the Bridegroom (Eph. 5:25-33), the sheep and the Shepherd (John 10). A member of the body cut off from the body would die. The marriage creates the union, but it takes daily love and devotion to maintain the communion. The shepherd brings the sheep into the flock, but the sheep must follow the shepherd in order to have protection and provision.

The sooner we as believers discover that we are but branches, the better we will relate to the Lord; for we will know our own weakness and confess our need for His strength.

The key word is *abide;* it is used eleven times in verses 1-11 ("continue" in v. 9 and "remain" in v. 11). What does it mean to "abide"? It means to keep in fellowship with Christ so that His life can work in and through us to produce fruit. This certainly involves the Word of God and the confession of sin so that nothing hinders our communion with Him (v. 3). It also involves obeying Him because we love Him (vv. 9-10).

How can we tell when we are "abiding in Christ"? Is there a special feeling? No, but there are special evidences that appear and they are unmistakably clear. For one thing, when you are abiding in Christ, you produce fruit (v. 2). What that "fruit" is, we will discuss later. Also, you experience the Father's "pruning" so that you will bear more fruit (v. 2). The believer who is abiding in Christ has his prayers answered (v. 7) and experiences a deepening love for Christ and for other believers (vv. 9 and 12-13). He also experiences joy (v. 11).

This abiding relationship is natural to the branch and the

vine, but it must be cultivated in the Christian life. It is not automatic. Abiding in Christ demands worship, meditation on God's Word, prayer, sacrifice, and service—but what a joyful experience it is! Once you have begun to cultivate this deeper communion with Christ, you have no desire to return to the shallow life of the careless Christian.

(3) *The Vinedresser.* The vinedresser is in charge of caring for the vines, and Jesus said that this is the work of His Father. It is He who "purges" or prunes the branches so they will produce more fruit. Note the progression here: no fruit (v. 2), fruit, more fruit, much fruit (vv. 5 and 8). Many Christians pray that God will make them more fruitful, but they do not enjoy the pruning process that follows!

The vinedresser prunes the branches in two ways: he cuts away dead wood that can breed disease and insects, and he cuts away living tissue so that the life of the vine will not be so dissipated that the quality of the crop will be jeopardized. In fact, the vinedresser will even cut away whole bunches of grapes so that the rest of the crop will be of higher quality. God wants both quantity and quality.

This pruning process is the most important part of the whole enterprise, and the people who do it must be carefully trained or they can destroy an entire crop. Some vineyards invest two or three years in training the "pruners" so they know where to cut, how much to cut, and even at what angle to make the cut.

The greatest judgment God could bring to a believer would be to let him alone, let him have his own way. Because God loves us, He "prunes" us and encourages us to bear more fruit for His glory. If the branches could speak, they would confess that the pruning process hurts; but they would also rejoice that they will be able to produce more and better fruit.

Your Heavenly Father is never nearer to you than when He is pruning you. Sometimes He cuts away the dead wood that might cause trouble; but often He cuts off the living tissue that is robbing you of spiritual vigor. Pruning does not simply mean spiritual surgery that removes what is bad. It can also mean cutting away the good and the better so that we might enjoy the best. Yes, pruning hurts, but it also helps. We may not enjoy it, but we need it.

How does the Father prune us? Sometimes He simply uses the Word to convict and cleanse us. (The word translated "purge" in v. 2 is the same as "clean" in 13:10. See Ephesians 5:26-27.) Sometimes He must chasten us (Heb. 12:1-11). At the time, it hurts when He removes something precious from us; but as the "spiritual crop" is produced, we see that the Father knew what He was doing.

The more we abide in Christ, the more fruit we bear; and the more fruit we bear, the more the Father has to prune us so that the quality keeps up with the quantity. Left to itself, the branch might produce many clusters, but they will be inferior in quality. God is glorified by a bigger crop that is also a *better* crop.

(4) *The fruit.* The word *results* is often heard in conversations among Christian workers, but this is not actually a Bible concept. A machine can produce results, and so can a robot, but it takes *a living organism* to produce fruit. It takes time and cultivation to produce fruit; a good crop does not come overnight.

We must remember that the branches do not eat the fruit: others do. We are not producing fruit to please ourselves but to serve others. We should be the kind of people who "feed" others by our words and our works. "The lips of the righteous feed many" (Prov. 10:21).

Several different kinds of spiritual fruit are named in the Bible. We bear fruit when we win others to Christ (Rom. 1:13). We are a part of the harvest (John 4:35-38). As we grow in holiness and obedience, we are bearing fruit (Rom. 6:22). Paul considered Christian giving to be fruit from a dedicated life (Rom. 15:28). "The fruit of the Spirit" (Gal. 5:22-23) is the kind of Christian character that glorifies God and makes Christ real to others. Even our good works, our service, grow out of our abiding life (Col. 1:10). The praise that comes from our hearts and lips is actually fruit to the glory of God (Heb. 13:15).

Many of these things could be counterfeited by the flesh, but the deception would eventually be detected, for real spiritual fruit has in it *the seeds for more fruit.* Man-made results are dead and cannot reproduce themselves, but Spirit-produced fruit will go on reproducing from one life to another. There will be fruit—more fruit—much fruit.

A true branch, united with the vine, will always bear fruit. Not every branch bears a "bumper crop," just as not every field has a bumper harvest (Matt. 13:8, 23). But there is always fruit where there is life. If there is no fruit, the branch is worthless and it is cast away and burned. I do not believe our Lord is teaching here that true believers can lose their salvation, for this would contradict what He taught in John 6:37 and 10:27-30. It is unwise to build a theological doctrine on a parable or allegory. Jesus was teaching one main truth— the fruitful life of the believer—and we must not press the details too much. Just as an unfruitful branch is useless, so an unfruitful believer is useless; and both must be dealt with. It is a tragic thing for a once-fruitful believer to backslide and lose his privilege of fellowship and service. If anything, verse 6 describes divine· discipline rather than eternal destiny. "There is [for believers] a sin unto death" (1 John 5:16).

Our Lord had spoken about peace (14:27); now He mentions love and joy (vv. 9-11). Love, joy, and peace are the first three "fruit of the Spirit" named in Galatians 5:22-23. Our abiding in Christ certainly ought to produce His love, joy, and peace in our hearts. Because we love Him, we keep His commandments; and, as we keep His commandments, we abide in His love and experience it in a deeper way.

Several times in John's Gospel you will find Jesus speaking

about the Father's love for Him. We so emphasize God's love for the world and the church that we forget that the Father loves the Son. Because the Father does love the Son, He has put all things into the Son's hand (3:35) and has revealed all things to the Son (5:20). The Father loved the Son before the foundation of the world (17:24); He loved the Son when the Son died on the cross (10:17). The amazing thing is believers today can experience personally that same love! Jesus prayed "that the love with which Thou hast loved Me may be in them [the disciples and believers today]" (17:26).

As branches in the Vine, we have the privilege of abiding and the responsibility of bearing fruit. Now we turn to the second picture, that of *friends*.

2. Friends—We Must Obey (John 15:12-17)

Most of us have many acquaintances but very few friends, and even some of our friends may prove unfriendly or even unfaithful. What about Judas? "Yes, mine own familiar friend, in whom I trusted, which did eat of my bread, hath lifted up his heel against me" (Ps. 41:9). Even a devoted friend may fail us when we need him most. Peter, James, and John went to sleep in the garden when they should have been praying; and Peter even denied the Lord three times. Our friendship to each other and to the Lord is not perfect, but His friendship to us is perfect.

However, we must not interpret this word *friend* in a limited way, because the Greek word means "a friend at court." It describes that "inner circle" around a king or emperor. (In John 3:29, it refers to the "best man" at a wedding.) The "friends of the king" would be close to him and know his secrets, but they would also be subject to him and have to obey his commands. There is thus no conflict between being a friend and being a servant.

The perfect illustration of this in Scripture is Abraham, "the friend of God" (2 Chron. 20:7; Isa. 41:8; James 2:23), who was also the servant of God (Gen. 26:24). In Genesis 18, our Lord and two angels came to visit Abraham as they were on their way to investigate the sin of Sodom. Even though Abraham was nearly 100 years old, he interrupted his noonday rest, greeted the visitors, saw to their comfort, and fed them a lovely meal. In the first fifteen verses of this chapter, Abraham is on the move; and twice he refers to himself as a servant (vv. 3 and 5). Note that this old man "hastened" and "ran" and encouraged others to perform their work quickly, a perfect example of a servant. Nor did Abraham sit and eat with them. Like a true servant, he stood nearby, ready to do their bidding.

In the last half of the chapter, the atmosphere changes, and Abraham is quietly standing still, communing with the Lord. He is still a servant, but now he is being a friend. "Shall I hide from Abraham that which I do?" the Lord asked. As a friend of God, Abraham shared God's secrets.

It is this kind of a relationship that Jesus described when He called His disciples "friends." It was certainly a relationship of *love*, both for Him and for each other. The "friends of the King" could not compete with each other for attention or promotion. They were a part of the "inner circle," not to promote themselves, but to serve their King. What a rebuke this must have been to the selfish disciples who often argued over who was the greatest!

How is it possible for Jesus to *command* us to love one another? Can true love be commanded? You must keep in mind that Christian love is not basically a "feeling"; it is an act of the will. The proof of our love is not in our feelings but in our actions, even to the extent of laying down our lives for Christ and for one another (1 John 3:16). Jesus laid down His life for both His friends and His enemies! (Rom. 5:10) While the emotions are certainly involved, real Christian love is an act of the will. It means treating others the way God treats us.

So, our friendship with Christ involves love and obedience. But it also involves knowledge: He "lets us in on" His plans.

Indeed, He is our Master (John 13:13, 16), but He does not treat us as servants. He treats us as friends, *if* we do what He commands. Abraham was God's friend because he obeyed God (Gen. 18:19). If we have friendship with the world, we then experience enmity with God (James 4:1-4). Lot in Sodom was not called God's friend, even though Lot was a saved man (2 Peter 2:7). God told Abraham what He planned to do to the cities of the plain, and Abraham was able to intercede for Lot and his family.

It is interesting to note that, in John's Gospel, it is the servants who know what is going on! The servants at the wedding feast in Cana knew where the wine came from (2:9), and the nobleman's servants knew when the son was healed (4:51-53).

One of the greatest privileges we have as His friends is that of learning to know God better and "getting in on" God's secrets. I can never forget the impact on my own heart when I heard Dr. Oswald Sanders say to our Back to the Bible staff, "Each of us is as close to God as we choose to be." We are His friends, and we ought to be near the throne, listening to His Word, enjoying His intimacy, and obeying His commandments.

One day while he was a fugitive, David was near Bethlehem, his home city, and he longed for a drink of water from the well by the gate. Three of his mighty men were close enough to David to hear his sigh, and they risked their lives to bring their king the water that he wanted (2 Sam. 23:15-17). That is what it means to be a friend of the king.

In John 14:16, Jesus reminded the men that they had this privileged position only because of His grace. They did not choose Him; He chose them! He chose them out of the world (v. 19) and ordained them to do His will. Again, we find this important word *fruit.* As branches, we share His life and bear fruit; and as friends, we share His love and bear fruit. As branches, we are pruned by the Father; as friends, we are instructed by the Son, and His Word controls our lives.

The word *ordained* simply means "appointed." It refers to the act of setting someone apart for special service. We have graciously been chosen and set apart by the Lord in order to go into the world and bear fruit. He has sent us into the world (17:18) as His personal ambassadors to tell others about the King and His great salvation. When we witness to others and win them to Christ, this is bringing forth fruit to the glory of God.

As I mentioned before, the evidence of true sonship, discipleship (v. 8), and friendship (v. 15) is *fruit*. "Wherefore by their fruits ye shall know them" (Matt. 7:20). Where there is true fruit, it remains; man-made "results" eventually disappear. Fruit has in it the seed for more fruit, so the process goes on and on. Whatever is born of the Spirit of God has the mark of eternity upon it, and it will last.

Once again, Jesus brought up the privilege of prayer. The friends of the king certainly speak to their sovereign and share their burdens and needs with him. In the days of monarchies, it was considered a very special honor to be invited to speak to the king or queen; yet the friends of Jesus Christ can speak to Him at any time. The throne of grace is always available to them.

Verses 15 and 16 summarize for us what it means to be a friend of the King of kings. It is a humbling experience, for He chose us and we did not choose Him. We must keep this in mind lest we become proud and presumptuous. It means that we keep our ears open and listen to what He says to us. "Hast thou heard the secret of God?" (Job 15:8) "The secret of the Lord is with them that fear Him; and He will show them His covenant" (Ps. 25:14). We must be attentive and alert.

But the purpose for all of this is that we might obey Him and get His work done. The King has tasks that must be performed; and if we love Him, we will obey His commands. We will seek to bear fruit that will please Him and glorify the Father. Our joy should be to please Him.

Jesus closed this part of His message by reminding them (and us) of the most important commandment of all: love one another. There are dozens of "one another" statements in the New Testament, but all of them are summarized in "love one another." Jesus had already given this commandment to the Eleven (13:34-35), and now He has repeated it twice (15:12 and 17). It will be stated in one way or another many more times in the New Testament letters, especially by John in his first epistle. The friends of the King must not only love Him, but also one another. What joy it brings to His heart when He sees His friends loving one another and working together to obey His commands.

This study began in the vineyard and ended in the throneroom! The next study will take us to the battlefield where we experience the hatred of the lost world. If we are not abiding as branches and obeying as friends, we will never be able to face the opposition of the world. If we do not love one another, how can we ever hope to love lost men and women in the world? If we are not marching together as the friends of the King, we will never present a united front to the enemy.

"Without Me, ye can do nothing" (v. 5).

We are not simply handicapped or hindered. We are hopelessly paralyzed! We can do *nothing!*

But if we abide in Him, if we stay close to the throne, we can do *anything* that He commands us to do!

What a privilege—and what a responsibility!

4
What in the World
Is the Spirit Doing?

John 15:18–16:16

This long section—John 15:18–16:16—is tied together by two important themes: the opposition of the world against the church, and the ministry of the Spirit to and through the church. Our Lord had been talking about love (15:9-13, 17), but now He is talking about *hatred;* and He used the word seven times. It seems incredible that anyone would hate Jesus Christ and His people, but that is exactly what the situation is today; *and some of that hatred comes from religious people.* In a few hours, the religious leaders of Israel would be condemning their Messiah and crying out for His blood.

Our Lord had openly taught His disciples that one day persecution would come. He mentioned it in the Sermon on the Mount (Matt. 5:10-12, 44) and in His "commissioning sermon" when He sent out the disciples to minister (Matt. 10:16-23). In His sermon denouncing the Pharisees, Jesus openly said that they would persecute and kill God's servants (Matt. 23:34-35); and there was a similar warning given in His prophetic message on Mt. Olivet (Mark 13:9-13).

Throughout the Gospel of John, it is evident that the religious establishment not only opposed Jesus, but even sought to kill Him (5:16; 7:19, 25; 8:37, 59; 9:22; also note 11:8). As He continued His ministry, there was a tide of resentment, then hatred, and then open opposition against Him. So, the disciples should not have been surprised when Jesus brought up the subject of persecution, for they had heard Him warn them and they had seen Him face men's hatred during His ministry.

Until the Lord returns, or until we die, we must live in this hostile world and face continued opposition. How can we do it? What is the secret of victory? It is the presence and power of the Holy Spirit of God in our lives. This is the key section in the Upper Room message about the Holy Spirit and His ministry.

Before we study this passage and see the threefold ministry of the Spirit to the church in the world, we must pause to remind ourselves just who the Holy Spirit is. The Holy Spirit of God is a person; Jesus referred to the Spirit as "he" and not "it." The Holy Spirit has a mind (Rom. 8:27), a will (1 Cor. 12:11), and emotional feelings (Gal. 5:22-23).

In John 15:26 all three persons of the Godhead are mentioned: Jesus the Son will send the Spirit from the Father. Because the Holy Spirit is a person, and is God, it means that the Christian has God indwelling his body! If we did not have the Holy Spirit within, we would not be able to serve the Lord in this present evil world. We are to walk in the Spirit (Gal. 5:16), worship in the Spirit (Phil. 3:3), and witness in the Spirit (Acts 1:8).

Christians can stand and withstand in the midst of the world's hatred because of the special ministries of the Holy Spirit.

1. The Spirit as Comforter Encourages the Church (John 15:18–16:4)

We should begin by clarifying what Jesus means by "the world," because the term is used in Scripture in at least three different ways. It can mean *the created world* ("the world was made by Him"—John 1:10), the world of *humanity* ("For God so loved the world"—3:16), or *society apart from God and opposed to God.* We sometimes use the phrase "the world system" to define this special meaning.

For example, when you listen to the radio news, you may hear the announcer say, "And now the news from the world of sports!" Obviously, "the world of sports" is not a special country or planet where everybody lives who is connected in some way with sports. "The world of sports" refers to all the organizations, people, plans, activities, philosophies, etc. that are a part of sports. Some of these things are visible and some are invisible, but all of them are organized around one thing—sports.

"The world" from a Christian point of view involves all the people, plans, organizations, activities, philosophies, values, etc. that belong to society without God. Some of these things may be very cultural; others may be very corrupt; but all of them have their origins in the heart and mind of sinful man and promote what sinful man wants to enjoy and accomplish. As Christians, we must be careful not to love the world (1 John 2:15-17) or be conformed to the world (Rom. 12:1-2).

Jesus pulls no punches when He tells His disciples that their situation in the world will be serious and even dangerous. Note the progress in the world's opposition: hatred (15:18-19), persecution (15:20), excommunication, and even death (16:2). You can trace these stages of resistance as you read the Book of Acts.

Why does the world system, including the "religious world," hate the Christian, the one who believes on Jesus Christ and seeks to follow Him? Jesus gave several reasons.

First, *we are identified with Christ* (15:18 and 20). If they hated Him, they will also hate those of us who are identified with Him. In verse 20, Jesus quoted the statement He had made earlier (13:16), and the logic of it is clear. He is the Master; we are the servants. He is greater than we are, so He must receive the praise and glory. But the world will not give

Him praise and glory! The world hates Him, and therefore the world must hate us. If with all of His greatness and perfection, Jesus does not escape persecution, what hope is there for us with our imperfections?

This principle is seen in some of the other images of the relationship between Christ and His own. He is the Shepherd and we are the sheep; and when they attack the Shepherd, it affects the sheep (Matt. 26:31). He is the Master (Teacher) and we are the disciples, the learners. But it is encouraging to know that when God's people are persecuted, our Lord enters into their suffering, for He is the Head of the Body and we are the members. "Saul, Saul, why persecutest thou Me?" (Acts 9:4) Anything that the enemy can do to us has already been done to Jesus Christ, and He is "with us" as we suffer.

Second, *we do not belong to the world* (v. 19). When we trusted Christ, we moved into a new spiritual position: we are now "in Christ" and "out of the world." To be sure, we are *in* the world physically, but not *of* the world spiritually. Now that we are "partakers of the heavenly calling" (Heb. 3:1) we are no longer interested in the treasures or pleasures of sin in this world. This does not mean that we are isolated from reality or insulated from the world's needs, so "heavenly minded that we are no earthly good." Rather, it means that we look at the things of earth from heaven's point of view.

The world system functions on the basis of conformity. As long as a person follows the fads and fashions and accepts the values of the world, he or she will "get along." But the Christian refuses to be "conformed to this world" (Rom. 12:2). The believer is a "new creation" (2 Cor. 5:17) and no longer wants to live the "old life" (1 Peter 4:1-4). We are the light of the world and the salt of the earth (Matt. 5:13-16), but a dark world does not want light and a decaying world does not want salt! In other words, the believer is not just "out of step"; he is out of place! (See John 17:14 and 16, and 1 John 4:5.)

There is a third reason why the world hates the believer: *the world is spiritually ignorant and blind* (v. 21). If you had asked the religious leaders in Jerusalem if they knew the God they were seeking to defend, they would have said, "Of course we know Him! Israel has known the true God for centuries!" But Jesus said that they *did not* know the Father and, therefore they could not know the Son (see 16:3). The religious leaders knew a great deal about Jehovah God and could quote chapter and verse to defend their doctrines, but they did not personally know God.

This was not a new theme for our Lord to discuss, because He had mentioned it before to the religious leaders who opposed Him. "Ye neither know Me, nor My Father; if ye had known Me, ye should have known My Father also" (8:19). "Yet ye have not known Him; but I know Him" (8:55). Jesus had taught them the Word and had demonstrated His deity in miraculous signs and a godly walk; and yet the religious leaders of the nation were blind to His identity: "The world knew Him not" (1:10).

The religious world today claims to know God, but it does not want to bow the knee to Jesus Christ as the Son of God and the only Saviour of the world. Satan has blinded their minds (2 Cor. 4:3-4) and sin has blinded their hearts (Eph. 4:17-19). Like Saul of Tarsus, they are so convinced that their "religion" and "righteousness" are satisfactory that *in the name of that religion* they persecute God's people!

There is a fourth reason: *the world will not be honest about its own sin* (vv. 22-24). Once again, Jesus emphasized His words and His works. We have seen this emphasis throughout the Gospel of John (3:2; 5:36-38; 10:24-27; 14:10-11). The people had no excuse ("cloak") for their sin. They had seen His works and heard His word, but they would not admit the truth. All of the evidence had been presented, but they were not honest enough to receive it and act upon it.

This statement is parallel to what Jesus told the Pharisees after He had healed the blind man (9:39-41). They had to admit that Jesus had healed the man born blind, but they would not follow the evidence to its logical conclusion and put *their* trust in Him. Jesus told them that they were the ones who were blind! But since they admitted that they had seen a miracle, this made their sin even worse. They were not sinning in ignorance; they were sinning against a flood of light. Why? Because that light revealed their own sin and they did not want to face their sin honestly. Their attitude was similar to that described in 2 Peter 3:5—"For this they *willingly* are ignorant of . . . " (italics mine).

How does the Holy Spirit encourage believers when they are experiencing the hatred and opposition of the world? It is primarily through the Word of God. For one thing, the Spirit reminds us that this opposition is clearly expressed by various writers in the Scriptures. In verse 25, Jesus quoted Psalm 35:19 and Psalm 69:4. The Word assured Him that the hatred of the world was not because of anything He had done to deliberately incite such opposition. We today can turn to verses like Philippians 1:28-30, 2 Timothy 2:9-12, Hebrews 12:3-4, and 1 Peter 4:12ff. We also have the encouraging words of our Lord found in the Gospels.

The Spirit also witnesses to us and through us during times of persecution (vv. 26-27). He reminds us that what we are experiencing is "the fellowship of His [Christ's] sufferings" (Phil. 3:10) and that it is a privilege to bear reproach for His name. (Read *carefully* 1 Peter 4:12-19.)

Times of persecution have always been for the church times of proclamation and witness. We must be "ready always to give an answer" when unsaved people attack us (1 Peter 3:15). The Spirit witnesses to us so that we can witness to the world (Mark 13:11). Apart from the power of the Spirit of God, we cannot give a clear witness for Christ (Acts 1:8).

There is no reason for the believer to stumble ("be offended," 16:1) when the world stokes up the furnace of persecution. He should expect persecution, if only because his Lord told him it was coming. (Note especially 13:19 and 14:29 where the Lord warned His disciples in advance.) Furthermore, they must not stumble when this persecution comes from religious people who actually think they are serving God. The word translated "service" in 16:2 means "priestly service." This statement is certainly a description of Saul of Tarsus, who thought he was serving God by destroying the church (see Acts 7:57–8:3, 22:3-4, and 26:9-12).

It is tragic when "religious" people persecute and murder in the name of God. While it is true that "the blood of the martyrs is the seed of the church" (Tertullian), it is also true that their blood is the stain on the pages of history.

2. The Spirit as Reprover Witnesses through the Church (John 16:5-11)

For three years, Jesus had been with them to protect them from attack; but now He was about to leave them. He had told them this earlier in the evening (John 13:33), and Peter had asked Him where He was going (13:36). However, Peter's question revealed more concern about *himself* than about the Lord Jesus! Also, his question centered on the immediate, not the ultimate. It was necessary for Jesus to explain why it was important *for them* that He return to the Father.

The major reason, of course, is that the Holy Spirit might come to empower the church for life and witness. Also, the ascended Saviour would be able to intercede for His people at the heavenly throne of grace. With all of their faults, the disciples dearly loved their Master; and it was difficult for them to grasp these new truths.

It is important to note that the Spirit comes *to the church* and not to the world. This means that He works in and through the church. The Holy Spirit does not minister in a vacuum. Just as the Son of God had to have a body in order to do His work on earth, so the Spirit of God needs a body to accomplish His ministries; and that body is the church. Our bodies are His tools and temples, and He wants to use us to glorify Christ and to witness to a lost world.

Sometimes we hear people pray, "Lord, send Your Spirit to speak to the lost! May the Spirit go from heart to heart." Such praying is no doubt sincere, but is it biblical? The Spirit does not "float" in some ghostly way up and down the rows of a church building, seeking to win the lost. The Holy Spirit works through the people in whom He lives. When the Holy Spirit came at Pentecost, He empowered Peter to preach; and the preaching of the Word brought conviction to those who heard.

The key word here is *reprove* (v. 8). It is a legal word that means "to bring to light, to expose, to refute, to convict and convince." It could be translated "pronounce the verdict." The world may think that it is judging Christians, but it is the Christians who are passing judgment on the world as they witness to Jesus Christ! Believers are the witnesses, the Holy Spirit is the "prosecuting attorney," and the unsaved are the guilty prisoners. However, the purpose of this indictment is not to condemn but to bring salvation.

The Holy Spirit convicts the world of one particular sin, the sin of *unbelief*. The law of God and the conscience of man will convict the sinner of his *sins* (plural) specifically; but it is the work of the Spirit, through the witness of the believers, to expose the unbelief of the lost world. After all, it is unbelief that condemns the lost sinner (John 3:18-21), not the committing of individual sins. A person could "clean up his life" and quit his or her bad habits and still be lost and go to hell.

The Spirit also convicts the sinner of *righteousness,* not *un*righteousness. Whose righteousness? The righteousness of Jesus Christ, the perfect Lamb of God. The world would not receive the Son of God (1:10), so He has returned to the Father. When He was here on earth, He was accused by men of being a blasphemer, a lawbreaker, a deceiver, and even a demoniac. The Spirit of God reveals the Saviour in the Word and in this way glorifies Him (vv. 13-14). The Spirit also reveals Christ in the lives of believers. The world cannot receive or see the Spirit of God, but they can see what He does as they watch the lives of dedicated believers.

The Spirit convicts the lost sinner of *judgment.* Do not confuse this statement with Acts 24:25 ("of righteousness, temperance, and judgment to come"). Jesus was referring to His judgment of Satan that was effected by His death on the cross (John 12:31). Satan is the prince of this world, but he is a defeated prince. Satan has already been judged and the verdict announced. All that must take place is the executing of the sentence, and that will occur when Jesus returns.

When a lost sinner is truly under conviction, he will see the folly and evil of unbelief; he will confess that he does not measure up to the righteousness of Christ; and he will realize that he is under condemnation because he belongs to the world and the devil (Eph. 2:1-3). The only person who can rescue him from such a horrible situation is Jesus Christ, the Son of God. There can be no conversion without conviction, and there can be no conviction apart from the Spirit of God using the Word of God in the witness of a faithful child of God.

Witnessing is a great privilege, but it is also a serious responsibility. It is a matter of life or death! How we need to depend on the Holy Spirit to guide us to the right persons, give us the right words, and enable us patiently to glorify Jesus Christ.

3. The Spirit as Teacher Guides the Church (John 16:12-15)

Our Lord was always careful to give His disciples the right amount of truth at the best time for them to receive it. This is always the mark of a great teacher. The Holy Spirit is our Teacher today, and He follows that same principle: He teaches us the truths we need to know, when we need them and when we are ready to receive them.

When you compare John 14:26 with 16:13, you see the

wonderful way that God arranged for the writing of the New Testament Scriptures. The Spirit would remind them of what Jesus had taught them; this gives us the four Gospels. The Spirit would also "guide" them into all truth; and this would result in the epistles. "He will show you things to come" refers to the prophetic Scriptures, especially the Book of Revelation.

It is essential that we see that the work of the Spirit of God is never divorced from Jesus Christ or the Word of God. "He shall testify of Me" (15:26); "He shall glorify Me" (16:14). People who claim that the Spirit of God led them to do things contrary to the example of Christ or the teaching of the Word are mistaken and are being led astray by Satan. Jesus is the truth (14:6), and the Word is truth (17:17), and the Holy Spirit is "the Spirit of truth." Where the Holy Spirit is at work, there must be truth.

The phrase "He [the Spirit] shall not speak of Himself" (v. 13) does not mean that the Spirit never refers to Himself, for when He wrote the Bible, the Spirit often mentioned Himself. Rather, it means that He does not speak apart from the Father and the Son; He does not "manufacture" a different message. You have the entire Godhead mentioned in verse 13, because the Spirit of God does not ignore either the Father or the Son. They work harmoniously together.

The teaching of the Spirit through the apostles was not different from the teaching of the Spirit through Jesus Christ. Some theologians like to contrast the "Christianity of Christ" with the "Christianity of Paul." They claim that Paul "ruined" Christianity by making it so theological and complicating the "simple message" of Jesus Christ. What a sad interpretation this is. What Jesus said in 14:26 and 16:13 completely refutes this false teaching. The one and selfsame Holy Spirit communicated the truths found in the four Gospels, the epistles, and the Book of Revelation; and He also wrote the history and doctrine found in Acts.

It is the ministry of the Spirit to enrich us with the treasures of God's truth. He enlightens us with God's truth and enriches us with God's treasures. The Word of God is a rich mine of gold, silver, and precious jewels (Prov. 3:13-15; 8:10-21). What a joy it is to have the Spirit illumine His Word and reveal Jesus Christ to us!

We do not study the Word of God in order to "argue religion" with people, or to show off our grasp of spiritual things. We study the Word to see Jesus Christ, to know God better, to glorify Him in our lives. As we witness in this hostile world, the Spirit uses the Word He has taught us; and we share Jesus Christ with the lost. It is our job to witness; it is the Spirit's job to convict.

Perhaps some of us need to quit acting like prosecuting attorneys—or judges—so that the Spirit can use us as faithful witnesses.

5
Let There Be Joy!

John 16:16-33

This section—John 16:16-33—concludes the Upper Room discourse and deals primarily with the emotions of the disciples. They were sorrowing, they were confused about some of Jesus' teaching, and they were afraid. It is an encouragement to me to know that the disciples were real men with real problems, yet the Lord was able to use them. We sometimes get the false impression that these men were different from us, especially endowed with spiritual knowledge and courage; but such was not the case. They were human!

One of the recurring themes in this section is *joy* (vv. 20-22, 24, 33). The Eleven were certainly not experiencing much joy that night! But what Jesus said to them eventually made a difference in their lives, just as it can make a difference in our lives today. Tenderly and patiently, our Lord explained how His people can have joy in their lives.

1. There Is a Principle to Grasp (John 16:16-22)
The principle is simply this: God brings joy to our lives, not by substitution, but by transformation. His illustration of the woman giving birth makes this clear. *The same baby that*

caused the pain also caused the joy. In birth, God does not substitute something else to relieve the mother's pain. Instead, He uses what is there already but transforms it.

Every parent knows what it is like to have an unhappy child because a toy is broken or a playmate has gone home. The parent can do one of two things: substitute something else for the broken toy or absent friend, or transform the situation into a new experience for the unhappy child. If Mother always gets a new toy for the child each time a toy is broken, that child will grow up expecting every problem to be solved by substitution. If Mother always phones another playmate and invites him or her over, the child will grow up expecting people to come to his rescue whenever there is a crisis. The result either way is a spoiled child who will not be able to cope with reality.

The way of substitution for solving problems is the way of immaturity. The way of transformation is the way of faith and maturity. We cannot mature emotionally or spiritually if somebody is always replacing our broken toys.

Jesus did not say that the mother's sorrow (pain) was replaced by joy, but that the sorrow was transformed into joy. The same baby that caused the pain also caused the joy! And so it is in the Christian life: God takes seemingly impossible situations, adds the miracle of His grace, and transforms trial into triumph and sorrow into joy. "The Lord thy God turned the curse into a blessing" (Deut. 23:5; see Neh. 13:2).

Joseph's brothers sold him as a slave, and Potiphar put him into prison as a criminal; but God transformed that hopeless situation of defeat into victory. Egypt's persecution of Israel only caused them to multiply and prosper the more. King Saul's murderous pursuit of David only made him more a man of God and helped produce the psalms that encourage our hearts today. Even Jesus took the cross, a symbol of defeat and shame, and transformed it into a symbol of victory and glory.

Now that we understand this principle, we can better understand the problems and questions of the disciples.

In verse 16, Jesus announced that in a little while, they would not see Him; then, in a little while, they would see Him. It was a deliberately puzzling statement (v. 25, He spoke in proverbs ["dark sayings"]) and the disciples did not understand. This also encourages me as I study my Bible and find statements that I cannot understand. Even the disciples had their hours of spiritual ignorance!

What did Jesus mean? Possibly He was talking about the soon-to-occur events in connection with His death and resurrection. After His burial, they would not see Him for a little while; but then He would rise from the dead and they would see Him again. He had told them on previous occasions that He would rise from the dead after three days, but His words did not sink into their minds and hearts.

However, I think that Jesus was speaking primarily about His return to the Father ("because I go to the Father"—v. 16). This ties in with verse 10, "because I go to My Father, and ye see Me no more." The disciples did not live to see the return of Christ, but they did die and see Him when they arrived in glory. In comparison to eternity, the time that the church has been awaiting the Lord's return has really been but "a little while" (see 2 Cor. 4:16-18). In fact, the phrase "a little while" is used in this very sense in Hebrews 10:37—"For yet a little while, and He that shall come will come, and will not tarry."

Instead of asking Jesus to explain His words, the men began to discuss it among themselves, almost as though they were embarrassed to admit their ignorance. However, you do not get very far by exchanging your ignorance! It is when we come to the Lord and ask for His help that we learn the important lessons of life.

Egypt was glad when Israel departed (Ps. 105:38), and the world was glad when Jesus Christ moved off the scene. Both the religious and political leaders of that day expected to see the early believers die out and the "Christian movement" disappear; but such was not the case. Jesus sent His Holy Spirit to His church, and the church is carrying the Word of His grace to the ends of the earth. The early believers even rejoiced when they were persecuted (Acts 5:41).

To the mother experiencing birth pains, every minute may seem an hour. Our concept of time changes with our feelings. Thirty minutes in the dentist chair may seem like hours, while hours fishing or dining with friends may seem like a very short time. The mother feels as though the birth is taking a long time, when really it may be only "a little while." When the baby has been born, pain is forgotten as joy fills her heart.

The world today does not want Jesus Christ or His church. The world is rejoicing while we are suffering, longing for our Lord to return. In fact, all of creation is suffering "birth pangs" because of sin, awaiting His return (Rom. 8:22). When the Bridegroom is away, the bride mourns (Matt. 9:15). But, in "a little while" He shall return and we shall go with Him to heaven to enjoy the Father's house.

While the immediate application may have been to the sorrowing hearts of the disciples, the ultimate application is to all of God's people as they await the coming of Jesus Christ. To us, it seems like a long wait; but God does not measure time as we do (see 2 Peter 3). But while we are waiting, we must deal with our trials and hurts on the basis of *transformation* and not *substitution*, if we expect to mature in the Christian life.

2. There Is a Promise to Believe (John 16:23-28)

The central theme of this paragraph is prayer: "ask, and ye shall receive, that your joy may be full" (v. 24). It is important to note that the text uses two different words for "ask," although they can be used interchangeably. The word used in verses 19, 23a, and 26 means "to ask a question" or "to ask a request." It is used when someone makes a request of someone equal. The word translated "ask" in 23b, 24, and 26b ("pray") means "to request something of a superior." This latter word was never used by Jesus in His prayer life because He is equal to the Father. We come as inferiors to God, asking for His blessing; but He came as the very Son of God, equal with the Father.

In verse 23, what period of time did Jesus mean by "in that day"? I think He was referring to the time after the coming of the Spirit. He promised them in verse 22 that He would see them again, and He kept His promise. He spent forty days with them after His resurrection, teaching them clearly the truths they needed to know in order to take His place and minister on earth (Acts 1:3ff). "That day" cannot refer to the day of His return for His church, because there is no evidence in Scripture that we shall pray to Him after we get to heaven.

Jesus knew that they wanted to ask Him a question (v. 19). He assured them that a day would soon come when they would not ask Him questions. Instead, they would pray to the Father and He would meet their needs. This was the promise that they desperately needed to believe: that the Father loved them and would hear their requests and meet their needs. While Jesus was on earth, He met all the needs of His disciples. Now He would return to the Father, but the Father would meet their needs. Here is the wonderful promise and privilege of prayer.

Our Lord had mentioned prayer many times in His ministry, and He had set the example for prayer in His own life. He was indeed a man of prayer. In His Upper Room message, Jesus emphasized prayer (14:12-14; 15:7 and 16; 16:23-26). He made it clear that believing prayer is one of the secrets of a fruitful Christian life.

In verses 25-27, Jesus explained that there would be a new situation because of His resurrection and ascension, and because of the coming of the Holy Spirit. He would no longer speak to them in terms that demanded spiritual insight for their understanding. He would speak to them plainly and reveal the Father to them. There in the Upper Room, He had used a number of symbolic images to get His message across:

the washing of their feet, the "Father's house," the vine and branches, and the birth of a baby. In the days that followed, these images would become clearer to the disciples as they would be taught by the Spirit of God.

The purpose of Bible study is not simply to understand profound truths, but to get to know the Father better. "I will show you plainly of the Father" (v. 25). If our reading and Bible study falls short of this, it does more harm than good.

There would be not only a new situation in teaching, but also a new situation in their praying. He had already intimated this in verse 23. Jesus would return to heaven to be with the Father, and there He would minister as our High Priest, making intercession for us (Rom. 8:34; Heb. 7:25). He would also minister as our Advocate (1 John 2:1). As our High Priest, Jesus gives us grace to keep us from sinning. As our Advocate, He restores us when we confess our sins. His ministry in heaven makes possible our ministry of witness on earth, through the power of the Spirit.

When you read the Book of Acts, you discover that the early church depended on prayer. They believed the promises of God and asked God for what they needed. It would do all of God's people good if they reviewed regularly what Jesus taught about prayer in this Upper Room discourse. There is indeed joy in praying and in receiving answers to prayer. There is joy in meeting the conditions Jesus has laid down for successful praying. I think it was George Müller who said that true prayer was not overcoming God's reluctance, but overcoming God's willingness.

There is joy in prayer, and there is joy in realizing the principle of *transformation.* Jesus shared a third kind of joy, the joy of sharing His victory over the world.

3. There Is a Position to Claim (John 16:29-33)
In verses 29-30, the disciples suddenly move out of their spiritual stupor and make a tremendous affirmation of faith.

First, they claimed to understand what He had been teaching them, although this claim was probably presumptuous, as their subsequent actions proved. They seemed unable to grasp the meaning of His promised resurrection. They were bewildered even after His resurrection as to the future of Israel (Acts 1:6ff). I am not criticizing them, because we today have just as many blind spots when it comes to understanding His Word. All I am suggesting is that their affirmation was a bit presumptuous.

They not only affirmed their understanding, but they also affirmed their faith and assurance. "Now we are sure . . . by this we believe. . . ." It was quite a statement of faith, and I believe the Lord accepted it. In His prayer recorded in the next chapter, Jesus told the Father about His disciples and reported on their spiritual condition (17:6-8). Certainly He knew their weaknesses, but He was quick to approve their growing evidences of faith and assurance.

But it is possible to have faith, understanding, and assurance *and still fail the Lord.* Unless we practice that faith, apply that understanding, and rest on that assurance, we will fail when the time of testing comes. That is what happened to the disciples, and Jesus warned them that it would happen.

He had already warned Peter that he would deny Him, but now He warned the entire band of disciples that they would all forsake Him. John does not quote the Old Testament prophecy (Zech. 13:7); it is quoted in Matthew 26:31. This statement from the Lord should have been a warning to Peter not to follow Jesus when He was arrested. "Let these go their way!" was our Lord's word in the garden (John 18:8). He knew that it was not safe for them to tarry.

Jesus has promised never to leave us alone (Matt. 28:20; Heb. 13:5); yet His own disciples left Him alone. Peter, James, and John went into the garden with Him, but then fell asleep. Jesus knew that the Father would be with Him. "I am not alone, but I and the Father that sent Me" (John 8:16). "And

He that sent Me is with Me. The Father hath not left Me alone" (8:29). What an encouragement it was to the Son to know that He was doing the Father's will and that He could depend on the Father's help.

At one point, however, Jesus did feel the absence of the Father: "My God, My God, why hast Thou forsaken Me?" (Matt. 27:46; Ps. 22:1) When He was made sin for us, He was separated from the Father. He was alone that we might never be alone. He was forsaken that we might never be forsaken.

Verse 33 is the summary and climax of the Upper Room message. Why did He give this message? So that the disciples might have peace in a world of tribulation. Note the contrast between "in Me" and "in the world." In Christ there is peace; in the world there is tribulation. This is the position we need to claim: we are *in Christ,* and therefore we can overcome the world and all of its hatred.

George Morrison defined peace as "the possession of adequate resources." In Jesus Christ, we have all the resources that we need. But peace depends also on appropriate relationships, because spiritual resources depend on spiritual relationships. "In Me" is the key. In ourselves, we have nothing; but "in Christ" we have all that we need.

Every believer is either *overcome* or an *overcomer.* "And this is the victory that overcometh the world, even our faith" (1 John 5:4). The world wants to overcome us; this is why Satan uses the world to persecute and pressure believers. The world wants us to conform; it does not want us to be different. When we yield ourselves to Christ and trust Him, He enables us to be overcomers. We must claim our spiritual position in Christ and believe Him for victory.

"Be of good cheer!" is one of our Lord's repeated statements of encouragement. Literally it means "Cheer up!" There is the "good cheer" of His pardon (Matt. 9:1-8), His power (Matt. 9:18-22), and His presence (Matt. 14:22-27). Here in John 16:33, He announces the "good cheer" of His victory over the world. We are overcomers because He has first overcome for us.

As we review this section, we can see how these three explanations our Lord gave all fit together. He revealed a wonderful principle—God transforms sorrow into joy. But this principle will not work in our lives unless we believe His promise and pray. God has ordained that His work is accomplished through believing prayer. But we will not be able to pray effectively if we do not claim our position as conquerors in Jesus Christ.

But verse 33 is also a preface to His great High Priestly prayer. He had taught them the Word; now He would pray for them. The Word and prayer must always go together (Acts 6:4). He used the word *world* nineteen times in this prayer, for in it He shows us how to overcome the world. He Himself was facing the hatred of the world *and the devil,* yet He would be able to endure the suffering and win the victory.

There is joy when we permit God to transform sorrow into joy. There is joy when God answers prayer. There is joy when we overcome the world.

Let there be joy!

6

The Prayer of the Overcomer

John 17

Most scholars who have sought to harmonize the accounts in the four Gospels have the Lord Jesus praying the prayer of John 17 in the Upper Room after He had finished His instructions to the disciples. Then He and the disciples sang the traditional Passover psalms, left the Upper Room, and headed for the Garden of Gethsemane where Jesus had been accustomed to meet with them and pray. (See Matthew 26:30-46 and Mark 14:26-42.)

Whether He prayed it in the Upper Room or en route to the garden, this much is sure: it is the greatest prayer ever prayed on earth and the greatest prayer recorded anywhere in Scripture. John 17 is certainly the "holy of holies" of the Gospel record, and we must approach this chapter in a spirit of humility and worship. To think that we are privileged to listen in as God the Son converses with His Father just as He is about to give His life as a ransom for sinners!

No matter what events occurred later that evening, this prayer makes it clear that Jesus was and is the Overcomer. He was not a "victim"; He was and is the Victor! "Be of good cheer," He had encouraged His disciples; "I have overcome the world" (16:33). The word *world* is used nineteen times in this prayer, so it is easy to see the connection between the prayer and John 16:33. If you and I will understand and apply the truths revealed in this profound prayer, it will enable us to be overcomers too.

The progression of thought in this prayer is not difficult to discover. Jesus first prayed for Himself and told the Father that His work on earth had been finished (vv. 1-5). Then He prayed for His disciples, that the Father would *keep them* and *sanctify them* (vv. 6-19). He closed His prayer by praying for you and me and the whole church, that we might be unified in Him and one day share His glory (vv. 20-26).

Why did Jesus pray this prayer? Certainly He was preparing Himself for the sufferings that lay ahead. As He contemplated the glory that the Father promised Him, He would receive new strength for His sacrifice (Heb. 12:1-3). But He also had His disciples in mind (John 17:13). What an encouragement this prayer should have been to them! He prayed about their security, their joy, their unity, and their future glory! He also prayed it for us today, so that we would know all that He has done for us and given to us, and all that He will do for us when we get to heaven.

In this prayer, our Lord declares four wonderful privileges we have as His children, privileges that help to make us overcomers.

1. We Share His Life (John 17:1-5)
Our Lord began this prayer by praying for Himself, but in praying for Himself, He was also praying for us. "A prayer for self is not by any means necessarily a selfish prayer," wrote Dr. R.A. Torrey, and an examination of Bible prayers shows that this is true. Our Lord's burden was the glory of God, and this glory would be realized in His finished work on the cross. The servant of God has every right to ask his Father for the help needed to glorify His name. "Hallowed be Thy name" is the

first petition in the Lord's Prayer (Matt. 6:9), and it is the first emphasis in this prayer.

"Father, the hour is come" reminds us of the many times in John's Gospel when "the hour" is mentioned, beginning at John 2:4 (see chapter 1 of this book). Jesus had lived on a "divine timetable" while on earth and He knew He was in the will of the Father. "My times are in Thy hand" (Ps. 31:15).

The important word *glory* is used five times in these verses, and we must carefully distinguish the various "glories" that Jesus mentions. In John 17:5, He referred to His preincarnate glory with the Father, the glory that He laid aside when He came to earth to be born, to serve, to suffer, and to die. In verse 4, He reported to the Father that His life and ministry on earth had glorified Him, because He (Jesus) had finished the work the Father gave Him to do. In verses 1 and 5, our Lord asked that His preincarnate glory be given to Him again, so that the Son might glorify the Father in His return to heaven.

The word *glory* is used eight times in this prayer, so it is an important theme. He glorified the Father in His miracles (2:11; 11:40), to be sure; but He brought the greatest glory to the Father through His sufferings and death (see 12:23-25 and 13:31-32). From the human point of view, Calvary was a revolting display of man's sin; but from the divine point of view, the cross revealed and magnified the grace and glory of God. Jesus anticipated His return to heaven when He said, "I have finished the work which Thou gavest Me to do" (v. 4). This "work" included His messages and miracles on earth (5:17-19), the training of the disciples for future service, and most of all, His sacrifice on the cross (Heb. 9:24-28; 10:11-18).

It is on the basis of this "finished work" that we as believers have the gift of eternal life (John 17:2-3). The word *give* is used in one form or another in this prayer at least seventeen times. Seven times Jesus states that believers are the Father's gift to His Son (vv. 2, 6, 9, 11, 12, 24). We are accustomed to think of Jesus as the Father's love gift to us (3:16), but the Lord affirms that believers are the Father's "love gift" to His beloved Son!

"Eternal (everlasting) life" is an important theme in John's Gospel; it is mentioned at least seventeen times. Eternal life is God's free gift to those who believe on His Son (3:15-16, 36; 6:47; 10:28). The Father gave His Son the authority to give eternal life to those whom the Father gave to the Son. From the human viewpoint, we receive the gift of eternal life when we believe on Jesus Christ. But from the divine viewpoint, we have already been given to the Son in divine election. This is a mystery that the human mind cannot fully understand or explain; we must accept it by faith.

But, what is "eternal life"? It is knowing God personally. Not just knowing *about* Him, but having a personal relationship with Him through faith in Jesus Christ. We cannot know the Father apart from the Son (14:6-11). It is not enough simply to "believe in God"; this will never save a lost soul from eternal hell. "The devils [demons] also believe, and tremble" (James 2:19). Our Lord's debate with the Jewish leaders (John 8:12ff) makes it clear that people may be devoutly religious and still not know God. Eternal life is not something we earn by character or conduct; it is a gift we receive by admitting we are sinners, repenting, and believing on Jesus Christ and Jesus Christ alone.

The Father answered His Son's request and gave Him the glory. There is in heaven today a glorified Man, the God-Man, Jesus Christ! Because He has been glorified in heaven, sinners can be saved on earth. Anyone who trusts Jesus Christ will receive the gift of eternal life.

Because we share His life, we are overcomers; for we also share His victory! "For whatsoever is born of God overcometh the world; and this is the victory that overcometh the world, even our faith" (1 John 5:4). When you were born the first time, you were born "in Adam" and were a loser. When you are born again through faith in Christ, you are born a winner!

Satan has tried to obscure the precious truth of the finished work of Jesus Christ, because he knows it is a basis for spiritual victory. "And they overcame him [Satan] by the blood of the Lamb" (Rev. 12:11). Don't let Satan rob you of your overcoming power through Christ's finished work.

2. We Know His Name (John 17:6-12)

Christ has given His own eternal life (v. 2), but He has also given them the revelation of the Father's name (v. 6). The Old Testament Jew knew his God as "Jehovah," the great I AM (Ex. 3:11-14). Jesus took this sacred name "I AM" and made it meaningful to His disciples: "I am the Bread of Life" (John 6:35); "I am the Light of the world" (8:12); "I am the Good Shepherd" (10:11); etc. In other words, Jesus revealed the Father's gracious name by showing His disciples that He was everything they needed.

But the Father's name includes much more than this, for Jesus also taught His disciples that God—the great I AM—was their Heavenly Father. The word *Father* is used fifty-three times in John 13–17, and 122 times in John's Gospel! In His messages to the Jews, Jesus made it clear that the Father sent Him, that He was equal to the Father, and that His words and works came from the Father. It was a clear claim to deity, but they refused to believe.

In the Bible, "name" refers to "nature," because names so often were given to reveal something special about the nature of the person bearing the name. Jacob was a schemer, and his name comes from a Hebrew root that means "to take by the heel," i.e., to trip up, to deceive (Gen. 25:26). The name Isaac means "laughter" (Gen. 21:6) because he brought joy to Abraham and Sarah. Even the name Jesus reveals that He is the Saviour (Matt. 1:21).

"I have manifested Thy name" means "I have revealed the nature of God." One of the ministries of the Son was to declare the Father (John 1:18). The Greek word translated "declared" means, "to unfold, to lead, to show the way." Jesus did not instantly reveal the Father, in a blaze of blinding glory, because His disciples could not have endured that kind of experience. Gradually, by His words and His deeds, He revealed to them the nature of God, as they were able to bear it (16:12).

The emphasis in this section is on the safety of the believer; God keeps His own (vv. 11-12). Our safety depends on the nature of God, not our own character or conduct. When He was on earth, Jesus kept His disciples and they could depend on Him. "I kept them in Thy name" (v. 12). If the limited Saviour, in a human body, could keep His own while He was on earth, should He not be able to keep them now that He is glorified in heaven? He and the Father, together with the Holy Spirit, are surely able to guard and secure God's people!

Furthermore, God's people are the Father's gift to His Son. Would the Father present His Son with a gift that would not last? The disciples had belonged to the Father by creation and by covenant (they were Jews), but now they belonged to the Son. How precious we are in His sight! How He watches over us and even now prays for us! Whenever you feel as though the Lord has forgotten you, or that His love seems far away, read Romans 8:28-39—and rejoice!

Our security rests in another fact: we are here to glorify Him (John 17:10). With all of their failures and faults, the disciples still receive this word of commendation: "I am glorified in them." Would it bring glory to God if one of His own, who trusted in the Saviour, did not make it to heaven? Certainly not! This was Moses' argument when the nation of Israel sinned: "Wherefore should the Egyptians speak, and say, 'For mischief did He bring them out, to slay them in the mountains, and to consume them from the face of the earth?'" (Ex. 32:12) Certainly God knows all things, so why save them at all if He knows they will fail along the way? Whatever God starts, He finishes (Phil. 1:6).

God has provided the divine resources for us to glorify Him

and be faithful. We have His Word (John 17:7-8), and His Word reveals to us all that we have in Jesus Christ. The Word gives us faith and assurance. We have the Son of God interceding for us (v. 9; Rom. 8:34; Heb. 4:14-16). Since the Father always answers the prayers of His Son (John 11:41-42), this intercessory ministry helps to keep us safe and secure.

We also have the fellowship of the church: "that they may be one, as we are" (v. 11). The New Testament knows nothing of isolated believers; wherever you find saints, you find them in fellowship. Why? Because God's people need each other. Jesus opened His Upper Room message by washing the disciples' feet and teaching them to minister to one another. In the hours that would follow, these men (including confident Peter!) would discover how weak they were and how much they needed each other's encouragement.

The believer, then, is secure in Christ for many reasons: the very nature of God, the nature of salvation, the glory of God, and the intercessory ministry of Christ. But what about Judas? Was he secure? How did he fall? Why did Jesus not keep him safe? For the simple reason that *Judas was never one of Christ's own.* Jesus faithfully kept all that the Father gave to Him, but Judas had never been given to Him by the Father. Judas was not a believer (6:64-71); he had never been cleansed (13:11); he had not been among the chosen (13:18); he had never been given to Christ (18:8-9).

No, Judas is not an example of a believer who "lost his salvation." He is an example of an unbeliever who *pretended to have salvation* but was finally exposed as a fraud. Jesus keeps all whom the Father gives to Him (10:26-30).

We are overcomers because we share His life. There is a third privilege that enables us to overcome.

3. We Have His Word (John 17:13-19)
"I have given them Thy Word" (v. 14, and see v. 8). The Word of God is the gift of God to us. The Father gave the words to His

Son (v. 8), and the Son gave them to His disciples who, in turn, have passed them along to us as they were inspired by the Spirit (2 Peter 1:20-21; 2 Tim. 3:16). The Word is divine in origin, a precious gift from heaven. We must never take God's Word for granted, for those who are overcomers know the Word and how to use it in daily life.

How does the Word of God enable us to overcome the world? To begin with, *it gives us joy* (John 17:13); and this inward joy gives us the strength to overcome (Neh. 8:10). We commonly think of Jesus Christ as "a man of sorrows" (Isa. 53:3), and indeed He was; but He was also a person of deep abiding joy. John 17:13 is the very heart of this prayer, *and its theme is joy!*

Jesus had referred to His joy already (15:11) and had explained that joy comes by transformation and not substitution (16:20-22). Joy also comes from answered prayer (16:23-24). Now He makes it clear that joy comes from the Word also. The believer does not find his joy in the world but in the Word. Like John the Baptist, we should rejoice greatly when we hear the Bridegroom's voice! (3:29)

We must never picture Jesus going around with a long face and a melancholy disposition. He was a man of joy and He revealed that joy to others. His joy was not the fleeting levity of a sinful world but the abiding enjoyment of the Father and the Word. He did not depend on outward circumstances but on inward spiritual resources that were hidden from the world. This is the kind of joy He wants us to have, and we can have it through His Word. "Thy word was unto me the joy and rejoicing of mine heart" (Jer. 15:16)./"I have rejoiced in the way of Thy testimonies, as much as in all riches" (Ps. 119:14)./"I rejoice at Thy word, as one that findeth great spoil" (Ps. 119:162).

The Word not only imparts the joy of the Lord, but it also *assures us of His love* (John 17:14). The world hates us, but we are able to confront this hatred with God's own love, a love imparted to us by the Spirit through the Word. The world hates us because we do not belong to its system (15:18-19) and will not be conformed to its practices and standards (Rom. 12:2). The Word reveals to us what the world is really like; the Word exposes the world's deceptions and dangerous devices.

The world competes for the Father's love (1 John 2:15-17), but the Word of God enables us to enjoy the Father's love. One of the first steps toward a worldly life is the neglect of the Word of God. D.L. Moody wrote in the front of his Bible, "This book will keep you from sin or sin will keep you from this book." Just as the pillar of fire was darkness to the Egyptians but light to Israel, so God's Word is our light in this dark world, but the world cannot understand the things of God (Ex. 14:20; 1 Cor. 2:12-16).

The Word of God not only brings us God's joy and love, but it also imparts God's power for holy living (John 17:15-17). The burden of our Lord's prayer in verses 6-12 was *security*, but here it is *sanctity*, practical holy living to the glory of God. We are *in* the world but not *of* the world, and we must not live *like* the world. Sometimes we think it would be easier if we were "out of the world," but this is not true. Wherever we go, we take our own sinful self with us, and the powers of darkness will follow us. I have met people who have gone into "spiritual isolation" in order to become more holy, only to discover that it does not work.

True sanctification (being set apart for God) comes through the ministry of the Word of God. "Now ye are clean through the word which I have spoken unto you" (15:3). When you were saved, you were set apart for God. As you grow in your faith, you are more and more experiencing sanctification. You love sin less and you love God more. You want to serve Him and be a blessing to others. All of this comes through the Word.

God's truth has been given to us in three "editions": His Word is truth (v. 17); His Son is the truth (14:6); and His Spirit is the truth (1 John 5:6). We need all three if we are to experience true sanctification, a sanctification that touches every part of our inner person. With the mind, we *learn* God's truth through the Word. With the heart, we *love* God's truth, His Son. With the will, we yield to the Spirit and *live* God's truth day by day. It takes all three for a balanced experience of sanctification.

It is not enough merely to study the Bible and learn a great deal of doctrinal truth. We must also love Jesus Christ more as we learn all that He is and all He has done for us. Learning and loving should lead to living, allowing the Spirit of God to enable us to obey His Word. This is how we glorify Him in this present evil world.

The Word gives us joy, love, and power to live a holy life. It also gives us what we need to serve Him as witnesses in this world (John 17:18-19). Sanctification is not for the purpose of selfish enjoyment or boasting; it is so that we might represent Christ in this world and win others to Him. Jesus set Himself apart for us, and now He has set us apart for Him. The Father sent Him into the world, and now He sends us into the world. We are people "under orders" and we had better obey! Jesus is now "set apart" in heaven, praying for us, that our witness will bear fruit as many repent of their sins and turn to the Lord.

How can we be overcome by the world when we have the Word of God to enlighten us, enable us, and encourage us?

4. We Share His Glory (John 17:20-26)

Here our Lord focuses our attention on the future. He begins to pray for us today, for the whole church throughout all ages. He has already prayed about security and sanctity; now the burden of His prayer is *unity.* He is concerned that His people experience a spiritual unity that is like the oneness of the Father and the Son. Christians may belong to different fellowships, but they all belong to the Lord and to each other.

The disciples had often exhibited a spirit of selfishness,

competition, and disunity; and this must have broken the Saviour's heart. I wonder how He feels when He sees the condition of the church today! The Puritan preacher Thomas Brooks wrote: "Discord and division become no Christian. For wolves to worry the lambs is no wonder, but for one lamb to worry another, this is unnatural and monstrous."

What is the basis for true Christian unity? The person and work of Jesus Christ and His glory (vv. 2-5). He has already given His glory to us, and He promises that we will further experience that glory when we get to heaven! All true believers have God's glory within, no matter what they may look like on the outside. Christian harmony is not based on the externals of the flesh but the internals and eternals of the Spirit in the inner person. We must look beyond the elements of our first birth—race, color, abilities, etc.—and build our fellowship on the essentials of our new birth.

We already possess His glory within (v. 22, and note Romans 8:29), and one day we shall behold His glory in heaven (v. 24). As we grow in the Lord, the glory within begins to grow and to reveal itself in what we say and do and the way we say and do it. People do not see us and glorify us; they see the Lord and glorify Him (Matt. 5:16; 1 Cor. 6:19-20).

One of the things that most impresses the world is the way Christians love each other and live together in harmony. It is this witness that our Lord wants in the world "that the world may believe that Thou hast sent Me" (John 17:21). The lost world cannot see God, but they can see Christians; and what they see in us is what they will believe about God. If they see love and unity, they will believe that God is love. If they see hatred and division, they will reject the message of the Gospel.

Jesus has assured us that some will believe because of our witness (v. 20), but we must make sure that our witness is true and loving. Some Christians are prosecuting attorneys and judges instead of faithful witnesses, and this only turns lost sinners away from the Saviour.

There is every reason why believers should love one another and live in unity. We trust the same Saviour and share the same glory. We will one day enjoy the same heaven! We belong to the same Father and seek to do the same work, witnessing to a lost world that Jesus Christ alone saves from sin. We believe the same truth, even though we may have different views of minor doctrinal matters; and we follow the same example that Jesus set for His people, to live a holy life. Yes, believers do have their differences; but we have much more in common, and this should encourage us to love one another and promote true spiritual unity.

I have often used John 17:24 as a text for funeral meditations. How do we know that Christians go to heaven? Because of the price that Jesus paid (3:14-16), and the promise that Jesus made (14:1-6), and the prayer that Jesus prayed (17:24). The Father always answers His Son's prayers, so we know that believers who die do go to heaven to behold the glory of God.

In verses 25 and 26, there are no petitions. Jesus simply reports to His Father about the ministry in the world, and He makes several declarations that are important to us. He declares that the world does not know the Father, but that we believers know Him because the Son has revealed the Father to us. The world certainly has many opportunities to get to know the Father, but it prefers to go on in blindness and hardness of heart. Our task as Christians is to bear witness to the lost world and share God's saving message.

He also declares the importance of truth and love in the church. Believers know God's name (nature) and even share in that divine nature. Jesus makes it clear that *truth* and *love* must go together (see Eph. 4:15). It has well been said that truth without love is brutality, but love without truth is hypocrisy. The mind grows by taking in truth, but the heart grows by giving out in love. Knowledge alone can lead to pride (1 Cor. 8:1), and love alone can lead to wrong decisions (see Phil. 1:9-10). Christian love must not be blind!

As you review this prayer, you see the spiritual priorities that were in the Saviour's heart: the glory of God; the sanctity of God's people; the unity of the church; the ministry of sharing the Gospel with a lost world. We today would be wise to focus on these same priorities.

One day, each of us will have to give an account of his or her ministry. It is a solemn thought that we shall stand before the judgment seat of Christ and give our "final report."

I trust that we will be able to say, "I have glorified Thee on the earth; I have finished the work which Thou gavest me to do" (John 17:4).

7
Guilt and Grace
in the Garden

John 18:1-27

The private ministry of our Lord with His disciples has now ended, and the public drama of redemption is about to begin. Man will do his worst, and God will respond with His very best. "But where sin abounded, grace did much more abound" (Rom. 5:20).

Perhaps the best way to see the truths in John 18:1-27, and grasp the lessons they convey, is to pay attention to the symbolism that is involved. John's Gospel is saturated with symbols, some more obvious than others; and these symbols convey some important spiritual truths. There are five such symbols in this section.

1. The Garden—Obedience (John 18:1)

The Kidron Valley is located east of Jerusalem, between the city wall and the Mount of Olives; and the Garden of Gethsemane is on the western slope of Olivet. Jesus often went to this garden with His disciples, no doubt to rest, meditate, and pray (Luke 22:39). Jerusalem was filled with pilgrims attending the Passover, and Jesus would want to get away from the crowded city to a private place. He knew that Judas would come for

Him there, and He was ready.

Human history began in a garden (Gen. 2:8ff), and the first sin of man was committed in that garden. The first Adam disobeyed God and was cast out of the garden, but the Last Adam (1 Cor. 15:45) was obedient as He went into the Garden of Gethsemane. In a garden, the first Adam brought sin and death to mankind; but Jesus, by His obedience, brought righteousness and life to all who will trust Him. He was "obedient unto death, even the death of the cross" (Phil. 2:8).

History will one day end in another garden, the heavenly city that John describes in Revelation 21 and 22. In that garden, there will be no more death and no more curse. The river of the water of life will flow ceaselessly and the tree of life will produce bountiful fruit. Eden was the garden of disobedience and sin; Gethsemane was the garden of obedience and submission; and heaven shall be the eternal garden of delight and satisfaction, to the glory of God.

The name *Gethsemane* means "oil press." Even today there are ancient olive trees in Gethsemane, although certainly not the ones that were there in Jesus' day. The olives would be picked and put into the press for their oil. What a picture of suffering! So our Lord would go through the "oil press" and the "winepress" (Isa. 63:3) and taste our judgment for us.

The Brook Kidron is also significant. The name means "dusky, gloomy," referring to the dark waters that were often stained by the blood from the temple sacrifices. Our Lord and His disciples were about to go through "dark waters," and Jesus would experience the "waves and billows" of God's wrath (Ps. 42:7; also note Jonah 2:3).

The Kidron had special historical significance, for King David crossed the Kidron when he was rejected by his nation and betrayed by his own son, Absalom (2 Sam. 15; also note John 18:23). Jesus had been rejected by His people and at that very moment was being betrayed by one of His own disciples! It is interesting that David's treacherous counselor Ahithophel hanged himself (2 Sam. 17:23), and David's treacherous son Absalom was caught in a tree and killed while hanging there (2 Sam. 18:9-17). Judas, of course, went out and hanged himself (Matt. 27:3-10).

Jesus fully knew what lay before Him, yet He went to the garden in obedience to the Father's will. He left eight of the men near the entrance, and took Peter, James, and John and went to another part of the garden to pray (Matt. 26:36-46; Mark 14:32-42). His human soul longed for the kind of encouragement and companionship they could give Him at this critical hour; but, alas, they went to sleep! It was easy for the men to boast about their devotion to Christ, but when the test came, they failed miserably. Before we judge them too severely, however, we had better examine our own hearts.

2. The Kiss—Treachery (John 18:2-9)

Judas had lived with the Lord Jesus for perhaps three years, and had listened to Him teach; yet he knew very little about Him. The traitor actually brought a company of temple guards, armed with swords and clubs! (Matt. 26:55) Just think of the privileges Judas despised and the opportunities he wasted! The word *band* in John 18:3 could be translated "cohort." A Roman cohort was a tenth of a legion, and this would be 600 men! It is not likely that Judas brought that many to the garden, but apparently a full cohort was made available to him had he needed it. Did he not realize that the Lamb of God would meekly submit and that there would be no need to battle?

Jesus was in full control; He knew what would happen (see 13:1, 3, 11, and 16:19). Judas expected some kind of deception, so he arranged to identify Jesus by kissing Him (Matt. 26:48-49). But Jesus shocked both Judas and the arresting officers by boldly presenting Himself to them. He had nothing to fear and nothing to hide; He would *willingly* lay down His life for His sheep. Furthermore, by surrendering to the officers,

Jesus helped to protect His disciples. He kept them safe not only spiritually (17:11-12) but also physically.

Why did the arresting soldiers draw back and fall to the ground when Jesus told them, "I am He"? The Jews present would be struck by His "I AM" statement, an affirmation of deity. The Romans, who were in the majority, would be struck by His bearing, for it was obvious that He was in command. It was an emotionally-charged situation, and we do not know what Judas had told them about Jesus to help prepare them for this confrontation. The Jewish leaders had tried to have Jesus arrested before and always without success. The band was prepared for conflict, and when they met with surrender and calm, they were overwhelmed.

Perhaps it was a manifestation of divine power, or an exhibition of the majesty of Jesus Christ. "When the wicked, even mine enemies and my foes, came upon me to eat up my flesh, they stumbled and fell" (Ps. 27:2).

Judas' kiss, which was given repeatedly to the Lord, was certainly one of the basest acts of treachery recorded anywhere in sacred or secular history. In that day, a kiss was a sign of affection and devotion. Members of the family kissed each other in meeting and in parting, but Judas was not a member of God's family. Disciples greeted a rabbi by kissing him; it was a sign of devotion and obedience. But Judas was not truly a disciple of Jesus Christ, though he belonged to the disciple band. In the garden, Judas stood with the enemy, not with Jesus' friends!

When people today pretend to know and love the Lord, they are committing the sin of Judas. It is bad enough to betray Christ, but to do it with *a kiss*, a sign of affection, is the basest treachery of all. It was born in the pit of hell.

3. The Sword—Rebellion (John 18:10)

All of the disciples had courageously affirmed their devotion to Christ (Matt. 26:35), and Peter decided to prove it; so he quickly drew out a small sword and started to fight! He certainly misunderstood what Jesus had said about swords earlier that evening (Luke 22:35-38). He had warned them that from now on the situation would change, and men would treat them as transgressors. He was not suggesting that they use material swords to fight spiritual battles, but that they get a new mind-set and expect opposition and even danger. He had provided for them and protected them while He was with them on earth, but now He was returning to the Father. They would have to depend on the Holy Spirit and exercise wisdom. Peter apparently took His words literally and thought he was supposed to declare war!

Peter's sword symbolizes rebellion against the will of God. Peter should have known that Jesus would be arrested and that He would willingly surrender to His enemies (Matt. 16:21ff; 17:22-23; 20:17-19). Peter made every mistake possible! He fought the wrong enemy, used the wrong weapon, had the wrong motive, and accomplished the wrong result! He was openly resisting the will of God and hindering the work that Jesus came to accomplish! While we admire his courage and sincerity, it was certainly a demonstration of zeal without knowledge.

Why did Peter fail so miserably? For one thing, he had argued with the Lord when Jesus warned him that he would deny his Master that very night. Peter had slept when he should have been praying, and he talked when he should have been listening. He imitated the very enemies who came to arrest Jesus, for they too were armed with swords. Peter would discover that the sword of the Spirit is the weapon God's servants use in fighting their spiritual battles (Heb. 4:12; Eph. 6:17). He would use that sword at Pentecost and "slay" 3,000 souls!

Jesus did not need Peter's protection. He could have summoned legions of angels had He wanted to be delivered (Matt. 26:52-54). Luke tells us that Jesus healed Malchus' ear (22:51), which was certainly an act of grace on His part. It was gracious from Peter's point of view; for had He not healed Malchus, Peter might have been arrested and crucified! Peter was acting like one of the Jewish "zealots" and not like a disciple of Jesus Christ.

But it was also an act of grace toward Malchus. After all, he was only a servant; and why worry about what happens to a servant? He was also an enemy, standing with the men who came to arrest Jesus; so he ought to suffer! Is it possible that Malchus had actually laid hold of Jesus? We do not know; but if he did, he laid hands on the holy Son of God. However, our Lord did not judge Malchus, though he was a sinner deserving the wrath of God. Instead, He healed him! It was our Lord's last public miracle before the cross.

Keep in mind that this miracle reveals His grace toward us. If Jesus had the power to stun an armed mob and heal a severed ear, He could have saved Himself from arrest, trial, and death. *But He willingly submitted!* And He did it for us!

It is a sad thing when well-meaning but ignorant Christians take up the sword to "defend" the Lord Jesus Christ. Peter hurt Malchus, something no believer should do. Peter hurt the testimony of Christ and gave the false impression that His disciples hate their enemies and try to destroy them. (Note our Lord's reply to Pilate in John 18:36.)

4. The Cup—Submission (John 18:11-14)
Peter had a sword in his hand, but our Lord had a cup in His hand. Peter was resisting God's will but the Saviour was accepting God's will. Earlier, Jesus had prayed, "O My Father, if it be possible, let this cup pass from Me; nevertheless, not as I will, but as Thou wilt" (Matt. 26:39). The cup represented the suffering He would endure and the separation from the Father that He would experience on the cross. He prayed this prayer three times, evidence that His whole being was sensitive to the price He would pay for our salvation. His holy soul must

have been stirred to the depths when He contemplated being made sin!

The drinking of a cup is often used in Scripture to illustrate experiencing suffering and sorrow. When Babylon captured Jerusalem, the city had "drunken the dregs of the cup of trembling" (Isa. 51:17). Jeremiah pictured God's wrath against the nations as the pouring out of a cup (25:15-28). There is also a cup of consolation (Jer. 16:7) and the overflowing cup of joy (Ps. 23:5).

Jesus had compared His own sufferings to the drinking of a cup and the experiencing of a baptism (Matt. 20:22-23). When He instituted the supper, He compared the cup to His blood, shed for the remission of sins (Matt. 26:27-28). The image was a familiar one to His disciples, and it is not an unfamiliar image today. To "drink the cup" means to go through with a difficult experience; and "not my cup of tea" means saying no to a certain course of action. The fact that some trophies are designed like cups suggests that winners have been through demanding experiences and had to "swallow a lot."

Jesus was able to accept the cup because it was mixed by the Father and given to Him from the Father's hand. He did not resist the Father's will, because He came to do the Father's will and finish the work the Father gave Him to do. "I delight to do Thy will, O my God: yea, Thy law is within my heart" (Ps. 40:8). Since the Father had mixed and measured the contents of the cup, Jesus knew He had nothing to fear.

This is a good lesson to us: we need never fear the cups that the Father hands to us. To begin with, our Saviour has already drunk the cup before us, and we are only following in His steps. We need never fear what is in the cup because the Father has prepared it for us in love. If we ask for bread, He will never give us a stone; and the cup He prepares will never contain anything that will harm us. We may suffer pain and heartbreak, but He will eventually transform that suffering into glory.

Jesus deliberately gave Himself to His enemies. They bound Him and led Him to the house of Annas, which was not too far away. Annas had served as high priest until he was deposed by the Romans; now his son-in-law Caiaphas was the high priest. God had ordained that one man should serve as high priest for a lifetime, so it is easy to see that the Jewish religious establishment was in sad condition. It is generally believed that the high priest's family was in charge of the temple "business," and the fact that Jesus twice cleansed the temple must have aroused their anger against Him.

The "trial" before Annas was more like an informal hearing. It was illegal and it was brutal. Imagine a guard being allowed to strike a prisoner! Imagine a man not holding an office interrogating a prisoner!

Annas, of course, was looking for some kind of evidence on which to base an accusation that would lead to a verdict of capital punishment. What doctrine was Jesus teaching? Was it subversive? Jesus told him to ask the people who listened to Him, because He had said nothing secretly. In fact, Annas himself could have come and listened!

What about our Lord's disciples? Were they organized to overthrow the government? Did not one of them use his sword in the garden? Jesus was careful to say nothing about His disciples. Think of it: while Peter was in the courtyard denying his Lord, Jesus was on trial protecting Peter!

Jewish law demanded that witnesses be called before a prisoner was questioned. Annas defied this law, and eventually the council hired *false* witnesses. Jesus knew His rights ("bear witness of the evil"—John 18:23), but He did not insist on them. He is an example to us when we suffer wrongfully (1 Peter 2:19-25 and 4:12-19).

5. The Fire—Denial (John 18:15-27)
Jesus had predicted that Peter would deny Him three times (John 13:38; Matt. 26:34), but that he would be restored to

fellowship and service (Luke 22:32). Peter followed the crowd when he should have been fleeing (John 18:8, and see Matt. 26:30-32). Had he gone his way, he would never have denied the Lord. While we certainly admire his love and courage, we cannot agree with his actions; for he walked right into temptation. This is what Jesus warned him about in the garden (Matt. 26:41).

We do not know who the other disciple was who went with Peter into the courtyard of the home of the high priest. It was probably John, although it is difficult to understand how a fisherman could be acquainted with the high priest and his household. Was this "other disciple" possibly Nicodemus or Joseph of Arimathea? They would certainly have access to this home.

As you watch Peter, you see him gradually moving into the place of temptation and sin; and his actions parallel the description in Psalm 1:1. First, Peter walked "in the counsel of the ungodly" when he followed Jesus and went into the high priest's courtyard. Peter should have followed the counsel of Jesus and gotten out of there in a hurry! Then, Peter *stood* with the enemy by the fire (John 18:16, 18); and before long, he *sat* with the enemy (Luke 22:55). It was now too late and within a short time, he would deny his Lord three times.

First, a servant girl asked, "Art not thou also one of this man's disciples?" The Greek text indicates that she expected a negative answer, and that is what she got! Peter denied Christ by denying that he belonged to the band of disciples.

Peter remained by the fire, so it is no wonder that he was approached again. (That same night, Jesus had been perspiring as He had prayed in the garden!) Another servant girl asked the same question, again expecting a negative reply. The pronoun *they* in John 18:25 suggests that others in the circle around the fire took up the question and one by one hurled it at Peter.

The third question came from one of Malchus' relatives! The

Greek construction indicates that he expected an *affirmative* answer: "I saw you in the garden with Jesus, didn't I? Yes, I did!" After all, this man had gotten a good look at Peter because he was probably standing with Malchus when Jesus was arrested. Some of the bystanders took up the discussion (Matt. 26:73; Mark 14:70) so that Peter may have been surrounded by challengers.

At that point, Peter's resistance broke down completely. He began to "curse and swear" (Matt. 26:74). This does not mean that Peter let loose a volley of blasphemies, but rather that he put himself under a curse in order to emphasize his statement. He was on trial, so he put himself under an oath to convince his accusers that he was telling the truth.

It was at that point that the cock began to crow (John 18:27) just as Jesus had predicted (Matt. 26:34). There were four "watches": evening (6-9 P.M.), midnight (9-12), cockcrowing (12 midnight to 3 A.M.), and morning (3 A.M.-6 A.M.) (see Mark 13:35). The crowing of the cock reminded Peter of the Lord's words, and he went out and wept bitterly.

The crowing of the cock was assurance to Peter that Jesus was totally in control of the situation, even though He was bound and being harassed by the authorities. By controlling one bird, Jesus affirmed His sovereignty. According to Genesis 1:26, God gave man authority over the fish, the fowl, and the animals. Peter had seen Jesus exercise authority over the fish (Luke 5:1-11; Matt. 17:24-27) and the animals (Matt. 21:1-11); but now he recognized His authority over the birds.

But the cockcrowing was also an invitation to repentance. "When thou art converted, strengthen thy brethren" (Luke 22:32). Luke tells us that Jesus turned and looked at Peter (22:61), and this look of love broke Peter's heart. Peter had been a witness of Christ's sufferings (1 Peter 5:1), and by his own denials he added to those sufferings.

Keep in mind that the crowing of the cock was the announcement of the dawning of a new day! "Weeping may endure for a night, but joy cometh in the morning" (Ps. 30:5). It is worthwhile to contrast Peter and Judas. Peter wept over his sins and repented, while Judas admitted his sins but never really repented. Judas experienced remorse, not repentance. When Judas went out from the Upper Room, "it was night" (John 13:30); but when Peter went out to weep bitterly, there was the dawning of a new day. It is the contrast between godly sorrow that leads to true repentance, and the sorrow of the world (regret and remorse) that leads to death (2 Cor. 7:9-10). We will discover that Jesus restored Peter (John 21) and enabled him to serve with great power and blessing.

In the garden that night, you would find both guilt and grace. Peter was guilty of resisting God's will. Judas was guilty of the basest kind of treachery. The mob was guilty of rejecting the Son of God and treating Him as though He were the lowest kind of criminal.

But Jesus was gracious! Like King David, He crossed the Kidron, fully conscious that Judas was betraying Him. He went into the Garden of Gethsemane surrendered to the Father's will. He healed Malchus' ear. He protected His disciples. He yielded Himself into the hands of sinners that He might suffer and die for us.

> "Love so amazing, so divine,
> Demands my soul, my life, my all!"

What is in your hand today—the sword, or the cup?

8

"Suffered Under Pontius Pilate"

John 18:28–19:16

Long before the Jewish leaders had Jesus arrested in the garden, they had determined to kill Him (John 11:47-54). However, the Jewish council did not have the right to execute prisoners; so it was necessary to get the cooperation and approval of Rome. This meant a visit to the Roman procurator, Pontius Pilate.

There were three stages in both the Jewish "trial" and the Roman "trial." After His arrest, Jesus was taken to the home of Annas and there interrogated informally (18:12-14, 19-23). Annas hoped to get information that would implicate Jesus as an enemy of the state. He wanted to prove that both His doctrine ·and His disciples were anti-Roman, for then He would be worthy of death.

Stage two of the Jewish trial took place before Caiaphas and whatever members of the Sanhedrin the high priest could assemble at that hour of the night (Matt. 26:57-68; Mark 14:53-65). When Jesus confessed clearly that He was the Christ, the council found Him guilty of blasphemy and there-fore, according to their law, worthy of death. However, it was necessary for the council to meet early the next morning and give their verdict, since it was not considered legal to try capital cases at night. So, stage three of the Jewish trial took place as early as possible, and the leaders condemned Jesus to death (Matt. 27:1; Luke 22:66-71).

The three stages of the Roman trial were: the first appearance before Pilate (John 18:28-38), the appearance before Herod (Luke 23:6-12), and the second appearance before Pilate (John 18:39–19:16; and see Matt. 27:15-26, Mark 15:6-15, and Luke 23:13-25). As you can see, the Apostle John records only the interrogations by Annas and Pilate, and mentions Caiaphas only in passing. He focuses primarily on the Roman trial. By the time he wrote this Gospel, the Jewish nation had been scattered by Rome, Jerusalem had been destroyed, and Roman power was all that really mattered.

Pontius Pilate was in office from A.D. 26-36 and was not greatly liked by the Jews. He could be ruthless when he wanted to be (see Luke 13:1-2), but he also understood the Jewish power structures and knew how to use them. His handling of the trial of Jesus reveals an indecisive man, a weak man, a compromising man. Rome's motto was, "Let justice be done though the heavens fall!" Pilate was not concerned about justice; his only concern was to protect himself, his job, and Rome. Alas, he failed in all three!

As you read John's account, you see Pilate seeking to find some "loophole" that will please both sides. He is afraid of the crowd, but then he grows more and more afraid of the prisoner! At least three times he announced that Jesus was not guilty of any crime (Luke 23:14; John 19:4; Luke 23:22; John 19:6). Yet he refused to release Him!

The Roman "trial," conducted by Pilate, revolved around four key questions.

1. "What Is the Accusation?" (John 18:28-32)

As soon as the Sanhedrin had voted to condemn Jesus, the officers took Him to the palace where Pilate was living during the Passover season. It was customary for the Roman governor to be in Jerusalem during Passover in case there were any outbursts of Jewish nationalism. The religious leaders did not hesitate to condemn an innocent man, but they were careful not to be defiled by walking on Gentile ground! It would be tragic to be ceremonially defiled during the seven days of Passover!

It was logical for Pilate to ask for the official accusation. Instead of stating the charges clearly, the Jewish leaders "beat around the bush" and probably made the astute politician suspicious. Luke 23:2 lists three "official charges": (1) He led the nation astray; (2) He opposed paying tribute to Caesar; and (3) He claimed to be the Jewish Messiah and King.

Pilate was not anxious to get involved in a Jewish court case, especially at Passover; so he tried to evade the issue. After all, if the prisoner was creating problems for the Jews, let the Jews try Him under their own law. Rome had permitted the Jews to retain a certain amount of jurisdiction, especially in matters relating to their religious laws and customs. (See Acts 18:12-16 for another example.)

But had the Jews *alone* judged Jesus and found Him guilty, He would have been killed by stoning; and God had determined that the Son would be crucified (see John 3:14; 8:28; 12:32-33). Jesus was to bear the curse of the law and become a curse for us; and in order to do this, He had to hang on a tree (Deut. 21:22-23; Gal. 3:13). The fact that the Romans allowed the Jews to stone Stephen to death indicates that Rome was lenient with the Sanhedrin on some capital cases (Acts 7:57-60).

When you seriously consider the three accusations against Jesus, you quickly see that they were completely unsupportable. For one thing, He had not "subverted" the nation, either politically or religiously. Of course, He had publicly denounced the Pharisees and their hypocritical religious system, but He was not the first one—or the only one—to do that. Jesus had blessed the nation and brought them new hope. The fact that some of the militant Jews saw in Him a potential king (John 6:15) was not our Lord's fault, and He fled from all such political demonstrations.

As for opposing paying tribute to Caesar, *He taught just the opposite!* "Render therefore unto Caesar the things which are Caesar's," He said, "and unto God the things that are God's" (Matt. 22:21).

He did claim to be King but not in a political sense. Even His own disciples did not fully understand these truths until after His resurrection (Acts 1:1-8). It is no wonder the common people sometimes misunderstood Him (Luke 19:11). Of course, the Jewish religious leaders were groping for any piece of evidence they could find on which they could build a case; and they were even willing to secure false witnesses!

2. "Are You the King of the Jews?" (John 18:33-38)

The question asking Jesus if he was king of the Jews is recorded by each of the Gospel writers. As Roman governor, Pilate would certainly be interested in the claims of any king. Messianic expectations always ran high at Passover season, and it would be easy for a Jewish pretender to incite the people into a riot or a rebellion against Rome. Pilate no doubt felt himself on safe ground when he asked about Christ's kingship.

However, he was not prepared for His answer. "It is as you say" (Matt. 27:11, NASB). But then Jesus added a question of His own: "Are you saying this on your own initiative, or did others tell you about Me?" (John 18:34, NASB) What was our Lord really asking? "What kind of a king do you have in mind? A Roman king or a Jewish king? A political king or a spiritual king?" Jesus was not evading the issue; He was forcing Pilate to clarify the matter *for his own sake.* After all, it was not Jesus that was on trial; it was Pilate!

If Pilate had a Roman king in mind, then Jesus could be considered a rebel. If the governor was thinking about a

Jewish kind of king, then political matters could be set aside. It is interesting that Pilate called Jesus "king" at least four times during the trial, and even used that title for the placard he hung on the cross (18:39; 19:3, 14, 15, 19).

Pilate's reply to Jesus showed what the Romans thought of the Jews: "Am I a Jew?" No doubt there was an obvious note of disdain and sarcasm in his voice. Jesus was not a prisoner because Pilate had arrested him, but because His own nation's leaders had arrested Him! Where there is smoke there must be fire; so Pilate asked, "What have You done?"

Graciously, Jesus consented to explain Himself and His kingdom. Yes, He admitted that He is a king; but His kingdom (reign) does not come from the authority of the world. The Jews were under Roman authority, and Pilate was under the authority of the emperor; but Jesus derived His authority from God. His kingdom is spiritual, in the hearts of His followers; and He does not depend on worldly or fleshly means to advance His cause. If His kingdom were from the world, by now His followers would have assembled an army and fought to release Him.

Jesus did not say that He had no kingdom in this world, or that He would never rule on earth. He does have a kingdom in this world, wherever there are people who have trusted Him and yielded to His sovereignty. One day He shall return and establish a righteous kingdom on earth (Dan. 7:13-28). Pilate's concern was the source of this kingdom: where did Jesus derive His authority?

In John 18:37, Jesus explained who He is and what kind of kingdom belonged to Him. Pilate probably did not grasp the significance of these profound words, but we today can discern some of the meaning Jesus had in mind. He was "born," which indicates His humanity; but He also "came into the world," which indicates His deity. The fact that Jesus came "into the world" means that He had existed before His birth at Bethlehem; and this is an important and repeated truth in

John's Gospel (1:9-10; 3:17, 19; 9:39; 10:36; 12:46; 16:28; 17:18).

But Jesus not only told Pilate of His origin; He also explained His ministry: to bear witness unto the truth. His was a spiritual kingdom of truth; and He won people to His cause, not through force, but through conviction and persuasion. He spoke the truth of God's Word, and all who were His people would respond to His call (see 8:47 and 10:27). Rome's weapon was the sword; but our Lord's weapon was the truth of God, the sword of the Spirit (Eph. 6:17).

We do not know with what attitude Pilate asked his now-famous question, "What is truth?" In his classic essay "Of Truth," Francis Bacon wrote, " 'What is Truth?' said jesting Pilate; and would not stay for an answer." But we are not certain that Pilate was jesting. Perhaps he was sincere. For centuries, Roman and Greek philosophers had discussed and debated this very question and had come to no settled conclusions. Whether Pilate was sneering or sighing as he asked the question, we do not know; so it would be unwise to pass judgment.

At least he had the courage to face the crowd and declare his verdict: "I find in Him no fault at all." But he did not get the response he desired, for the chief priests and elders only began to accuse Jesus all the more! (See Matt. 27:12-14.) Jesus was silent before His accusers (1 Peter 2:21-23) and this silence amazed Pilate. Could this king not even defend Himself? If He does not speak, how can anyone secure any evidence? Pilate faced a dilemma.

But the chief priests and elders solved his problem when they shouted that Jesus had stirred up the people even in Galilee (Luke 23:5). Galilee! That was Herod's responsibility, so why not send the prisoner to Herod, who was also in Jerusalem for the feast? Between John 18:38 and 39 you have the events recorded in Luke 23:6-12. Pilate's maneuver did not solve his problem, because Herod sent Jesus back! All that it accomplished was the healing of the breach between these two rulers. Pilate still had to deal with Jesus and the Jews.

3. "Shall I Release the King of the Jews?" (John 18:39–19:7)

The fact that Herod had found nothing worthy of death in Jesus encouraged Pilate to confront the Jewish leaders and seek to release the prisoner. He summoned the chief priests and rulers and told them that he found no guilt in Jesus, that Herod had found no guilt in Jesus, and that the next step would be to punish Jesus and release Him. The Jews had already made it clear that they wanted Jesus to die (18:31), but Pilate was feebly trying to do the noble thing.

Hoping to strengthen this suggestion, Pilate offered to bargain with the Jewish leaders. It was a custom at Passover for the governor to release a prisoner and please the Jews; so, why not release Jesus? Or, he could release Barabbas; but why would the Jews want Barabbas set free? After all, he was a robber (18:40), a notorious prisoner (Matt. 27:16), an insurrectionist and a murderer (Luke 23:19). Who would want *that* kind of a prisoner turned loose?

Incredible as it seems, the crowd asked for Barabbas! The people were persuaded by the chief priests and elders (Matt. 27:20) whose religious convictions did not motivate them toward justice and equity. National feelings always increased during Passover, and a vote *for* Barabbas was a vote *against* Rome. Even though Jesus had been a popular figure among the people, many of them no doubt were disappointed that He had not led a popular uprising to overthrow Rome. Perhaps they had even hoped that His "triumphal entry" a few days before would be the start of Jewish liberation.

There is no explaining how a mob chooses its heroes. No doubt many of the Jews admired Barabbas for his cunning and courage, and they rejoiced that he was fighting Rome. Had they honestly compared and contrasted the two "candidates," the people would have had to vote for Jesus Christ. But when a mob is manipulated by crafty leaders, in an atmosphere of patriotic fervor, it loses itself and starts to think with its feelings instead of its brains. Their condemning vote said nothing about the Son of God, but it said a great deal about them.

Never at a loss for an idea, Pilate tried a new approach—sympathy. The crowd had cried "Crucify Him!" (Mark 15:14) but perhaps they would be placated if Jesus were scourged. What man could behold a scourged prisoner and still want the victim crucified? The scourge was a leather whip, knotted and weighted with pieces of metal or bone; and many a prisoner never survived the whipping. It pains us to think that the sinless Son of God was subjected to such cruelty. He was innocent, yet He was treated as though He were guilty; and He did it for us. He was slapped in the face before Annas (John 18:22), and spat upon and beaten before Caiaphas and the council (Matt. 26:67). Pilate scourged Him and the soldiers smote Him (fs1John 19:1-3); and before they led Him to Calvary, the soldiers mocked Him and beat Him with a rod (Mark 15:19). How much He suffered for us!

Pilate had called Him "King of the Jews" (18:39), so the soldiers decided that the "king" should have a crown and a robe. The Jews had mocked His claim to being a prophet (Matt. 26:67-68), and now the Gentiles mocked His claim to being a King. The verb tenses in the Greek text in 19:3 indicate that the soldiers *repeatedly* came to Him, mocked Him, and beat Him with their hands. The forces of hell were having a heyday in Pilate's hall.

Sin had brought thorns and thistles into the world (Gen. 3:17-19), so it was only fitting that the Creator wear a crown of thorns as He bore the sins of the world on the cross. The very metal He had created and placed in the ground was used to make nails to pound through His hands and feet.

For the third time, Pilate went out to face the people

(John 18:29, 38; 19:4), this time bringing Jesus with him. Surely the sight of this scourged and humiliated prisoner would arouse some pity in their hearts; but it did not. For the second time, Pilate declared that he found no fault in Jesus, but his words only aroused their hateful passions more. "Behold the man!" carries the idea, "Look at this poor fellow! Hasn't He suffered enough? Take pity on Him and let me release Him." It was a noble effort on Pilate's part, but it failed.

The failure of Pilate's plan teaches us an important lesson: it takes more than human sentiment to bring the lost sinner to salvation. There is a view of the atonement called "the moral influence theory" that would fit right into the governor's approach. It states that the realization of our Lord's sufferings moves the heart of the sinner so that he turns from sin and begins to love God. It is purely subjective and has no bearing on the holiness of God or the importance of satisfying divine justice.

If any crowd should have been moved by pity, it was the Jewish crowd that awaited on Pilate. What nation has suffered more than the Jews? Here was one of their own, a Jewish prophet, suffering unjustly at the hands of the Romans, and the Jews did not repent or even show any touch of pity! If sinners who actually saw Christ in His suffering did not repent, what hope is there for people twenty centuries later who only read about His agonies?

The cross involves much more than an exhibition of innocent suffering. On that cross, the Son of God paid the price for the sins of the world and thereby declared the love of God and defended the holiness and justice of God. We are not saved by feeling pity for Jesus. We are saved by repenting of our sins and trusting Jesus, the sinless Substitute. "If Christ was not actually doing something by His death," wrote Dr. Leon Morris, "then we are confronted with a piece of showmanship, nothing more."

This does not mean that it is wrong for the believer to

contemplate the cross and meditate on Christ's sufferings. The familiar hymn "When I Survey the Wond'rous Cross" helps us realize afresh the price that Jesus paid for us, but we must not confuse sentimentality with true spiritual emotion. It is one thing to shed tears during a church service and quite something else to sacrifice, suffer, and serve after the meeting has ended. We do not simply contemplate the cross; we carry it.

For the third time, Pilate announced, "I find no fault in Him!" The crowd might well have shouted, "Then why did you have Him scourged?" Pilate's actions belied his words. He was a weak-willed man who, like many politicians, hoped to find a happy compromise that would please everybody. The Chinese teacher Confucius defined "cowardice" as "to know what is right and not do it."

The religious leaders were not at a loss for a powerful reply: "We have a law, and by our law He ought to die, because He made Himself the Son of God" (19:7). This statement is not found in the other Gospels (but see Matt. 26:63-64); however, it fits right into John's purpose in writing his Gospel (John 20:31).

4. "Where Are You From?" (John 19:8-16)

The Romans and Greeks had numerous myths about the gods coming to earth as men (note Acts 14:8-13), so it is likely that Pilate responded to the phrase "Son of God" with these stories in mind. Already the governor had been impressed by the words and demeanor of our Lord; he had never met a prisoner like Him before. Was He indeed a god come to earth? Did He have supernatural powers? No wonder Pilate was starting to be afraid! Also, Pilate's wife had sent him a strange message that he should have nothing to do with Jesus (Matt. 27:19). Jesus had even come into her dreams!

Why did Jesus not answer Pilate's question? Because He had already answered it (John 18:36-37). It is a basic spiritual principle that God does not reveal new truth to us if we fail to act upon the truth we already know. Furthermore, Pilate had already made it clear that he was not personally interested in spiritual truth. All he was concerned about was maintaining peace in Jerusalem as he tried to expedite the trial of Jesus of Nazareth. Pilate did not deserve an answer!

Fear and anger often go together. When we are afraid we are weak, we go the other extreme and try to appear strong. This is what Pilate did as he reminded Jesus of his Roman authority. But his statement did not demonstrate his power; it demonstrated his weakness. For if he had the authority to release Jesus, *why did he not do it?* He condemned himself with his own boastful words.

Of course, our Lord's silence before both Herod and Pilate was a fulfillment of Isaiah 53:7. Peter later used this as an example for suffering Christians to follow (1 Peter 2:18-23).

John 19:11 records our Lord's last words to Pilate, words that reveal His faith in the Father and His surrender to His will (see 1 Peter 2:23 and 4:19). All authority comes from God (Rom. 13:1ff). Jesus was able to surrender to Rome and the Jews because He was first of all yielded to God. Pilate was boasting about his authority (John 19:10), but Jesus reminded him that his so-called authority was only delegated to him from God. One day God would call him to account for the way he had used his privileges and responsibilities.

To whom was Jesus referring when He said "he that delivered Me up unto thee"? Certainly not God, because God does not and cannot sin. Jesus was referring to Caiaphas, the corrupt high priest who had long before determined that Jesus must die (11:47-54). Caiaphas knew the Scriptures and had been given every opportunity to examine the evidence. He had willfully closed his eyes and hardened his heart. He had seen to it that Jesus was not given a fair trial. It was his associates who were inciting the mob to cry, "Let Him be crucified!" Pilate was a spiritually blind pagan, but Caiaphas was a Jew who had a knowledge of Scripture. Therefore, it was Caiaphas, not Pilate, who had the greater sin.

What a dilemma Pilate was in! How would he go about investigating the claim that Jesus was "the Son of God"? And there was no evidence that He was a troublemaker or a seditionist. In a final burst of courage, Pilate tried to release Jesus. John does not tell us what steps Pilate took (the Greek text says "he kept seeking to release Him"), but they all failed. In fact, the crowd started to accuse Pilate of being a traitor to Caesar! This was too much for the governor, so he gave his official verdict and delivered Jesus to be crucified. Matthew tells us that Pilate washed his hands before the crowd (27:24), but this did not cleanse his heart. Alas, it was Pilate who was on trial, not Jesus!

It is likely that John used Roman time, so that "the sixth hour" would have been 6 o'clock in the morning. Mark tells us that Jesus was crucified "the third hour," which, in Jewish reckoning, would have been 9 o'clock in the morning. Since John wrote "*about* the sixth hour," we need not try to figure out why it took three hours to get Jesus from Pilate's hall to Calvary.

The "preparation" refers to the preparation for the Sabbath (see John 19:31) which would begin at sundown that day (Friday). Being the Passover Sabbath, it was an especially holy day. The religious leaders were more concerned about their traditions than they were knowing the truth and obeying the will of God. On a high and holy day, they crucified their own Messiah, Jesus the Son of God!

The crowd had the last word: "We have no king but Caesar!" "We will not have this man to reign over us!" (Luke 19:14) Well-meaning preachers have often said that the crowd that on Palm Sunday shouted "Hosannah!" turned right around and shouted "Crucify Him!" on Good Friday. However, it was two different crowds. The Palm Sunday crowd came primarily from Galilee where Jesus was very popular. The crowd at Pilate's hall was from Judea and Jerusalem where the religious leaders were very much in control. If the Galilean disciples had had their way, they would have revolted and delivered Jesus!

From the human standpoint, the trial of Jesus was the greatest crime and tragedy in history. From the divine viewpoint, it was the fulfillment of prophecy and the accomplishment of the will of God. The fact that God had planned all of this did not absolve the participants of their responsibility. In fact, at Pentecost, Peter put both ideas together in one statement! (Acts 2:23)

When Israel asked to have a king, and God gave them Saul, the nation rejected God the Father (1 Sam. 8:5-7). When they asked for Barabbas, they rejected God the Son. Today, they are rejecting the pleading of God the Holy Spirit (Acts 7:51; Rom. 10:21). Yet there will come a day when they shall see their King, believe, and be saved (Rev. 1:7; Matt. 24:30; Zech. 12:10-11).

Both the nation and the governor were on trial, and both failed miserably.

May we not fail!

> What will you do with Jesus?
> Neutral you cannot be.
> One day your heart will be asking,
> "What will He do with me?"

9
"Even the Death of the Cross"
John 19:17-42

The Apostle's Creed states it without embellishment: "He was crucified, dead, and buried. . . . " These three events are described in John 19:17-42, momentous events that we should understand not only from the historical point of view but also from the doctrinal. *What* happened is important; *why* it happened is also important, if you hope to go to heaven.

1. Crucified (John 19:17-27)

Pilate delivered Jesus to the chief priests; and they, with the help of the Roman soldiers, took Jesus to be crucified. "It was the most cruel and shameful of all punishments," said the Roman statesman-philosopher Cicero. "Let it never come near the body of a Roman citizen; nay, not even near his thoughts or eyes or ears."

Crucifixion probably had its origin among the Persians and Phoenicians, but it was the Romans who made special use of it. No Roman citizen could be crucified, although there were exceptions. This mode of capital punishment was reserved for the lowest kind of criminals, particularly those who promoted insurrection. Today, we think of the cross as a symbol of glory and victory; but in Pilate's day, the cross stood for the basest kind of rejection, shame, and suffering. It was Jesus who made the difference.

It was customary for the criminal to carry his cross, or at least the crossbeam, from the hall of judgment to the place of execution. Jesus began the mile-long walk carrying His cross, but He was relieved by Simon of Cyrene whom the Roman soldiers "drafted" to do the job. We do not know why Jesus was relieved of this burden; the Scriptures are silent. Was He too weak from the scourgings to carry the load? Was His weakness holding back the procession at a time when the Jews were anxious to get it over with so they could celebrate their Passover Sabbath? One thing is sure: the bearing of the cross was a mark of guilt; *and Jesus was not guilty* (see Mark 15:20-21 and Rom. 16:13).

It was also required that the criminal wear a placard announcing his crime. The only announcement recorded in the Gospels is the one that Pilate wrote: "This is Jesus of Nazareth the King of the Jews." The chief priests protested the title, but Pilate refused to change it. It was his final thrust against the Jewish religious establishment. He knew that the priests and elders envied Jesus and wanted to destroy Him (Matt. 27:18). A shrewd politician like Pilate well understood the workings of the Jewish religious establishment. He knew that his placard would insult and embarrass them, and that is exactly what he wanted.

The fact that this title was written in Hebrew (Aramaic), Greek, and Latin is significant. For one thing, it shows that our Lord was crucified in a place where many peoples and nations met, a cosmopolitan place. Hebrew is the language of religion, Greek of philosophy, and Latin of law; and all three combined to crucify the Son of God. But what He did on the cross, He did for the whole world! In this Gospel, John emphasizes the worldwide dimensions of the work of Christ. Without realizing it, Pilate wrote a "Gospel tract" when he prepared this title; for one of the thieves discovered that Jesus was King, and he asked entrance into His kingdom.

Jesus was crucified outside the city (Heb. 13:11-13) between two other victims, possibly associates of Barabbas. We do not know where our Saviour's cross stood. There have been so many changes in the topography of Jerusalem since A.D. 70 when Titus and the Romans destroyed it, that it is impossible to determine accurately either our Lord's route to the cross or where the cross stood. Pilgrims to the Holy Land today are shown both the Church of the Holy Sepulcher and "Gordon's Calvary" near the garden tomb.

The Hebrew word *Golgotha* means "cranium, skull"; Calvary is the Latin equivalent. We are not told why it had this peculiar name. Certainly Jewish people would not permit unclean skulls to be left at a place of public execution! For that matter, the bodies (with heads intact) were usually disposed of by burial (if the victims had friends) or by throwing them on the public garbage dump. "Gordon's Calvary" does resemble a skull, but did that terrain look like that 2,000 years ago?

That Jesus was crucified with two notorious thieves only added to the shame. But it also fulfilled Isaiah 53:12, "He was numbered with the transgressors." He was treated like a common criminal!

Modern executions are usually carried out in almost clinical privacy, but Jesus was nailed to a cross and hung up for everyone to see. It was Passover season and there were thousands of visitors in the city. The place of execution was outside the city where many people would pass. Jesus was a well-known figure, so His arrest and condemnation would be topics for discussion. It was natural for people to gather and watch the grim scene.

Of course, the soldiers had to be there; that was their job. At most Roman executions, a centurion would be assigned with four soldiers to assist him. Since Jesus was a popular teacher with many followers, Pilate may have assigned more guards to

Golgotha. It was the privilege of the soldiers to share whatever personal belongings the victims had; so they divided up all that Jesus owned—His personal clothing. He would have had a turban, a pair of sandals, an undergarment (the seamless robe), an outer garment, and a girdle. The four men took each of them a piece of clothing, and then they gambled for the seamless robe. This fulfilled Psalm 22:18.

John does not record it, but the other Gospel writers tell us that some of the people passing by reviled Jesus, no doubt at the instigation of the chief priests and scribes (Mark 15:29-32). When you read Psalm 22, you see how David used the image of *animals* to describe the people who persecuted our Lord: bulls (v. 12), lions (vv. 13, 21), and dogs (vv. 16, 20). When men reject their Lord, they become like animals.

A group of women, along with the Apostle John, stood near the cross. (Later, they would move farther away and join other friends of Jesus [Matt. 27:55-56; Mark 15:40-41].) John specifies four women: Mary, the mother of Jesus; His mother's sister, Salome, the mother of James and John; Mary, the wife of Clopas (Cleophas); and Mary Magdalene. It took courage to stand there in the midst of such hatred and ridicule, but their being there must have encouraged our Lord.

The first time we meet Mary in the Gospel of John, she is attending a wedding (2:1-11); now she is preparing for a burial. The hour had come! She was experiencing "the sword" that had been predicted years before (Luke 2:35). Her silence is significant; for if anyone could have rescued Jesus, it was His mother. All she had to do was announce that His claims were false—but she said nothing! What a testimony to the deity of Christ.

Jesus assured her of His love, and He gave His choicest disciple, who rested on His bosom, to be her adopted son and to care for her. Whether that moment John took Mary away from the scene and took her home, we do not know. We do know that he cared for her and that she was among the believers in the Upper Room as they awaited Pentecost (Acts 1:14). Even while He was performing the great work of redemption, Jesus was faithful to His responsibilities as a son. What an honor it was for John to take his Lord's place in Mary's life!

Do not confuse Mary Magdalene with the "sinful woman" described in Luke 7:36ff. Jesus had delivered Mary Magdalene from demons (Luke 8:2; Mark 16:9), and she used her resources to assist Jesus in His ministry. Salome had asked Jesus for thrones for her two sons (Matt. 20:20-29), and He had denied her request. You wonder what she was thinking about as she stood there and beheld Jesus dying on the cross. The scene must have rebuked her selfishness.

2. Dead (John 19:28-32)

Our Lord knew what was going on; He was fully in control as He obeyed the Father's will. He had refused to drink the pain-deadening wine that was always offered to those about to be crucified (Matt. 27:34). In order to fulfill the Scriptures (Ps. 69:21), He said, "I thirst." He was enduring real physical suffering, for He had a real human body. He had just emerged from three hours of darkness when He felt the wrath of God and separation from God (Matt. 27:45-49). When you combine darkness, thirst, and isolation, you have—hell! There were physical reasons for His thirst (Ps. 22:15), but there were also spiritual reasons (Ps. 42:1-2).

One of the soldiers took pity on Jesus and moistened His lips with the cheap vinegar wine the soldiers drank. We must not imagine Jesus hanging many feet up in the air, almost inaccessible. His feet were perhaps three or four feet from the ground, so it would be easy for the man to put a sponge at the end of a reed and give Jesus a drink. You and I today can "give Jesus a drink" by sharing what we have with those in need (Matt. 25:34-40).

Psalm 69 has strong messianic overtones. Note verse 3, "My

throat is dried." Verse 4 is referred to by Jesus in John 15:25, and verse 8 should be connected with John 7:3-5. Verse 9 is quoted in John 2:17, and verse 21 is referred to in John 19:28-29. Note the emphasis on "reproach" (vv. 7-10, 19-20) and the image of the "deep waters" (vv. 14-15, and see Luke 12:50).

Our Lord made seven statements while He was on the cross; they are known as "the seven words from the cross." First, He thought of others: those who crucified Him (Luke 23:34), the believing thief (Luke 23:39-43), and His mother (John 19:25-27). The central word had to do with His relationship to the Father (Matt. 27:45-49); and the last three statements focused on Himself: His body (John 19:28-29), His soul (John 19:30), (Isa. 53:10), and His spirit (Luke 23:46).

The drink of vinegar did not fully quench His thirst, but it did enable Him to utter that shout of triumph, in a loud voice, "It is finished!" In the Greek text, it is *tetelestai;* and it means, "It is finished, it stands finished, and it always will be finished!" While it is true that our Lord's sufferings were now finished, there is much more included in this dramatic word. Many of the Old Testament types and prophecies were now fulfilled, and the once-for-all sacrifice for sin had now been completed.

The word *tetelestai* is unfamiliar to us, but it was used by various people in everyday life in those days. A servant would use it when reporting to his or her master, "I have completed the work assigned to me" (see John 17:4). When a priest examined an animal sacrifice and found it faultless, this word would apply. Jesus, of course, is the perfect Lamb of God, without spot or blemish. When an artist completed a picture, or a writer a manuscript, he or she might say, "It is finished!" The death of Jesus on the cross "completes the picture" that God had been painting, the story that He had been writing, for centuries. Because of the cross, we understand the ceremonies and prophecies in the Old Testament.

Perhaps the most meaningful meaning of *tetelestai* was that used by the merchants: "the debt is paid in full!" When He gave Himself on the cross, Jesus fully met the righteous demands of a holy law; He paid our debt in full. None of the Old Testament sacrifices could take away sins; their blood only *covered* sin. But the Lamb of God shed His blood, and that blood can *take away* the sins of the world (John 1:29; Heb. 9:24-28).

There was once a rather eccentric evangelist named Alexander Wooten, who was approached by a flippant young man who asked, "What must I do to be saved?"

"It's too late!" Wooten replied, and went about his work.

The young man became alarmed. "Do you mean that it's too late for me to be saved?" he asked. "Is there nothing I can do?"

"Too late!" said Wooten. "*It's already been done!* The only thing you can do is believe."

The death of Jesus Christ is a major theme in the Gospel of John. It was announced by John the Baptist even before Jesus had officially begun His ministry (John 1:29, 35-36). Our Lord's first mention is in John 3:14, where the image is certainly that of crucifixion (and see 8:28 and 12:32). Jesus often spoke of "taking up the cross" (Matt. 10:38 and 16:24). After Peter's confession of faith, Jesus clearly announced that He would be killed (Matt. 16:21), and later He told the disciples that He would be crucified (Matt. 20:17-19).

In John's Gospel, you find a number of pictures of our Lord's death: the slaying of the lamb (1:29); the destroying of the temple (2:19); the lifting up of the serpent (3:14); the shepherd laying down his life for the sheep (10:11-18); and the planting of the seed in the ground (12:20-25). These pictures make it clear that Jesus' death was not an accident; it was a divine appointment. He was not murdered in the strictest sense: He willingly gave His life for us. His death was an atonement, not just an example. He actually accomplished the work of redemption on the cross.

Some unbelievers have invented the idea that Jesus did not

really die, that He only "swooned" on the cross and was then revived in the "cool tomb." But there are too many witnesses that Jesus Christ actually died: the centurion (Mark 15:44-45); all the Gospel writers; the angels (Matt. 28:5, 7); the Jews (Acts 5:28); Christ Himself (Luke 24:46; Rev. 1:18); and even the worshiping hosts in heaven (Rev. 5:9, 12). Of course, Paul, Peter, and John mention the death of Christ in their letters.

His death was voluntary: He willingly dismissed His spirit (John 19:30; and note 10:17-18). He "gave Himself" (Gal. 2:20). He offered Himself as a ransom (Mark 10:45), as a sacrifice to God (Eph. 5:2), and as a propitiation for sin (1 John 2:2). In Luke 9:31, His death is called a "decease," which in the Greek is "exodus," suggesting the Passover lamb and the deliverance from bondage. It will take eternity to reveal all that happened when Jesus Christ died on the cross.

3. Buried (John 19:31-42)

Two groups of people were involved in our Lord's burial: the Roman soldiers (John 19:31-37), and the Jewish believers (vv. 38-42). It was not unusual for victims to remain on the cross in a lingering death, so the Jewish religious leaders did all they could to hasten the death of Jesus and the two thieves. However, our Lord was in control; and He dismissed His spirit at "the ninth hour," which was 3 o'clock in the afternoon (see Matt. 27:45-50). The last three "words from the cross" were spoken within a short period of time just before He laid down His life.

It is remarkable that the Roman soldiers *did not do* what they were commanded to do—break the victims' legs—but they *did do* what they were not supposed to do—pierce the Saviour's side! In both matters, they fulfilled the very Word of God! The bones of the Passover lamb were not to be broken (Ex. 12:46; Num. 9:12; and note Ps. 34:20), so our Lord's bones were protected by the Lord. His side was to be pierced (Zech. 12:10; Rev. 1:7), so that was done by one of the soldiers.

John saw a special significance to the blood and water that

came from the wound in the side. For one thing, it proved that Jesus had a real body (see 1 John 1:1-4) and experienced a real death. By the time John wrote this book, there were false teachers in the church claiming that Jesus did not have a truly human body. There may also be a symbolic meaning: the blood speaks of our justification, the water of our sanctification and cleansing. The blood takes care of the guilt of sin; the water deals with the stain of sin. Some students connect John 19:34 with 1 John 5:6, but perhaps the connection is weak. In 1 John 5, John deals with evidence that Jesus Christ is God come in the flesh; and he presents three witnesses: the Spirit, the water, and the blood (5:6, 8). The Spirit relates to Pentecost, the water to His baptism, and the blood to His crucifixion. In each of these events, God made it clear that Jesus Christ is what He claimed to be, God come in the flesh. In fact, in John 19:35, the apostle makes it clear that the water and blood should encourage his readers to believe that Jesus is the Christ (see 20:31).

When the soldiers were through with their gruesome work, our Lord's friends took over; and from that point on, as far as the record is concerned, no unbelievers touched the body of Jesus. God had prepared two high-ranking men to prepare His body for burial and to place it in a proper tomb. Had Joseph and Nicodemus not been there, it is likely that the body of Jesus would have been "carried off to some obscure and accursed ditch," as James Stalker states in his classic *The Trial and Death of Jesus Christ.* If the friends of any victims appeared, the Romans were only too happy to give them the bodies and get them off their hands.

When you assemble the data available about Joseph of Arimathea, you learn that he was rich (Matt. 27:57), a prominent member of the Jewish council (Mark 15:43), a good and righteous man who had not consented to what the council did (Luke 23:50-51), a member of that "believing minority" of Jews who were praying for Messiah to come (Mark 15:43, and note Luke 2:25-38), and a disciple of Jesus Christ (John 19:38). It was he who asked for the body of Jesus and, with his friend Nicodemus, gave the Saviour decent burial.

But there are some mysteries about Joseph that perplex us and invite closer investigation. Why did he have a tomb so near to a place of execution? Most pious Jews wanted to be buried in the Holy City, but a rich man like Joseph could certainly afford a better site for his final resting place. Imagine his relatives coming to pay their respects and having to listen to the curses and cries of criminals on crosses not far away! (Note John 19:41.)

Matthew, Luke, and John all tell us that the tomb was new and had never been used. It was "his [Joseph's] own new tomb" (Matt. 27:60); he had hewn it out for himself. *Or did he hew it out for Jesus?*

John informs us that Joseph was a "secret disciple for fear of the Jews." The Greek word translated "secretly" is a perfect passive participle and could be translated "having been secreted." In Matthew 13:35, this same verb form is translated "have been kept secret." In other words, Joseph was God's "secret agent" in the Sanhedrin! From the human standpoint, Joseph kept "under cover" because he feared the Jews (John 7:13; 9:22; 12:42); but from the divine standpoint, he was being protected so he could be available to bury the body of Jesus.

We have already met Nicodemus in our study of John 1–12. Note that each time he is named, he is identified as the man who came to Jesus by night (3:1ff; 7:50-53). But the man who started off with confusion at night (John 3) ended up with open confession in the daylight! Nicodemus came out of the dark and into the light and, with Joseph, was not ashamed to publicly identify with Jesus Christ. Of course, when the two men touched His dead body, they defiled themselves and could not participate in Passover. But, what difference did it make? They had found the Lamb of God!

It seems evident that Joseph and Nicodemus carefully

planned their activities at Calvary. They certainly could not secure a tomb at the last minute, nor would they be able to purchase sixty-five pounds of costly spices so quickly during the Passover when many merchants would not be doing business. No sooner had Jesus died than Joseph went to Pilate and received permission to take the body. Nicodemus stayed at the cross to make sure nothing happened to his Lord's body. The two men might even have been waiting *in the new tomb,* with the spices and wrappings, ready for the moment when the Saviour would lay down His life.

Haste was important and the men worked quickly. They could not give Jesus' body the full ministry of washing and anointing that was traditional, but they did the best they could. It was important to get the body safely away from the Romans and the Jewish leaders. Of course, Mary of Bethany had already anointed His body for burial (John 12:1-8; Mark 14:8). Some of the other women watched the two men minister to Jesus, and they witnessed His burial (Matt. 27:61; Mark 15:47). They planned to return after the Sabbath and complete the burial procedures (Luke 23:55–24:1).

All of this raises the question, "How did Joseph and Nicodemus know to prepare for His burial?" What follows is only conjecture on my part but, to me, it seems reasonable.

When Nicodemus first visited Jesus, he was impressed with His miracles and His teachings; but he could not understand what it meant to be born again. Certainly after that interview, Nicodemus searched the Scriptures and asked God for guidance concerning these important spiritual matters.

At the critical council meeting recorded in John 7:45-53, Nicodemus boldly stood up and defended the Saviour! His associates ridiculed him for thinking that a prophet could come out of Galilee! "Search, and look!" they said—and that is exactly what Nicodemus did. It is likely that Joseph quietly joined him and revealed the fact that he too was more and more convinced that Jesus of Nazareth was indeed Israel's

Messiah, the Son of God.

As Nicodemus and Joseph searched the Old Testament, they would find the Messianic prophecies and discover that many of them had been fulfilled in Jesus Christ. Certainly they would see Him as the "Lamb of God" and conclude that He would be sacrificed at Passover. Jesus had already told Nicodemus that He would be "lifted up" (3:14), and this meant crucifixion. Since the Passover lambs were slain about 3 o'clock in the afternoon, the two men could know almost the exact time when God's Lamb would die on the cross! Surely they would read Isaiah 53 and notice verse 9—"And he made his grave with the wicked, and with the rich in his death." Jesus would be buried in a rich man's tomb!

Joseph arranged to have the tomb hewn out, and the men assembled the cloths and spices needed for the burial. They may have been hiding in the tomb all during the six hours of our Lord's agony on the cross. When they heard, "It is finished! Father, into Thy hands I commend My spirit!" they knew that He was dead; and they went to work. They boldly identified with Jesus Christ at a time when He seemed like a failure and His cause hopelessly defeated. As far as we know, of all the disciples, only John was with them at the cross.

The Sabbath was about to dawn. Jesus had finished the work of the "new creation" (2 Cor. 5:17), and now He would rest.

10
The Dawning of a New Day
John 20:1-18

If the Gospel of John were an ordinary biography, there would
be no chapter 20. I am an incurable reader of biographies,
and I notice that almost all of them conclude with the death
and burial of the subject. I have yet to read one that describes
the subject's resurrection from the dead! The fact that John
continued his account and shared the excitement of the resurrection miracle is proof that Jesus Christ is not like any other
man. He is, indeed, the Son of God.

The resurrection is an essential part of the Gospel message
(1 Cor. 15:1-8) and a key doctrine in the Christian faith. It
proves that Jesus Christ is the Son of God (Acts 2:32-36; Rom.
1:4) and that His atoning work on the cross has been completed and is effective (Rom. 4:24-25). The empty cross and the
empty tomb are God's "receipts" telling us that the debt has
been paid. Jesus Christ is not only the Saviour, but He is also
the Sanctifier (Rom. 6:4-10) and the Intercessor (Rom. 8:34).
One day He shall return as Judge (Acts 17:30-31).

From the very beginning, the enemies of the Lord tried to
deny the historic fact of the Resurrection. The Jewish leaders
claimed that the Lord's body had been stolen from the tomb.

This statement is absurd, for if the body was stolen by His followers, how did they do it? The tomb was guarded by Roman soldiers and the stone sealed by an official Roman seal. Furthermore, His disciples *did not believe* that He was to be raised from the dead; it was His enemies who remembered His words (Matt. 27:62-66). *They* certainly would not have taken the body! The last thing they wanted was anyone believing that Jesus had indeed risen from the dead. If His friends *could not* steal the body, and His enemies *would not,* then who took it?

Perhaps the disciples had "visions" of the risen Lord and interpreted them as evidences for the Resurrection. But they did not *expect* to see Him, and that is not the kind of psychological preparation from which hallucinations are made. And how could more than 500 people have the same hallucination at the same time? (1 Cor. 15:6)

Did the followers of our Lord perhaps go to the wrong tomb? Not likely. They carefully watched where He was buried (Matt. 27:61; Mark 15:47; Luke 23:55-57). They loved the Master and were not likely to get confused about His resting place. In fact, as the women approached the tomb, they were worried about who would roll back the heavy stone (Mark 16:1-3); so they were acquainted with the situation.

As to the foolish argument that Jesus did not die, but only swooned and was later revived, little need be said. It was proved by many witnesses that Jesus was dead when His body was taken from the cross. Later, He was seen alive by dependable witnesses. The only logical conclusion is that He kept His promise and arose from the dead.

But the glorious truth of the Resurrection was not understood immediately by even His closest followers. It gradually dawned upon these grieving people that their Master was not dead, but alive! And what a difference it made when the full realization of His resurrection took hold of them! For Mary Magdalene it meant moving from tears to joy (John 20:1-18); for the ten disciples it meant going from fear to courage

(20:19-23); and for Thomas it meant moving from doubt to assurance (20:24-31). With Mary, the emphasis is on love; with the ten, the emphasis is on hope; and with Thomas, the emphasis is on faith.

As we consider Mary Magdalene's experience that Lord's Day morning, we can see three stages in her comprehension of the truth of the Resurrection. Peter and John are also a part of this experience.

1. Faith Eclipsed (John 20:1-2)

Mary Magdalene and several other women agreed to go to the tomb early on the first day of the week, so that they might show their love for Christ in completing the burial preparations. Joseph of Arimathea and Nicodemus had been forced by circumstances to prepare His body hastily, and the women wanted to finish the task. Their great concern was how to get into the tomb. Perhaps the Roman soldiers would take pity on them and give them a hand.

What they did not know was that an earthquake had occurred and the stone had been rolled back by an angel! It seems that Mary Magdalene went ahead of the other women and got to the tomb first. When she saw the stone rolled away from the door of the tomb, she concluded that somebody had broken into the tomb and stolen the body of her Lord. We may criticize Mary for jumping to conclusions; but when you consider the circumstances, it is difficult to see how she would have reached any other conclusion. It was still dark, she was alone, and, like the other followers of Jesus, she did not believe that He would return from the dead.

She ran to give the news to Peter and John, who must have been living together at a place known to the other believers. Perhaps it was the Upper Room where they had met with Jesus. Mary's use of the pronoun "we" is interesting, for it included the other women who at that moment were discovering that Jesus was alive! (See Mark 16:1-8 and Luke 24:1-8.)

The women left the tomb and carried the angels' message to the other disciples.

It is significant that the first witnesses of the resurrection of Christ were *believing women.* Among the Jews in that day, the testimony of women was not held in high regard. "It is better that the words of the Law be burned," said the rabbis, "than be delivered to a woman." But these Christian women had a greater message than that of the Law, for they knew that their Saviour was alive.

Mary's faith was not extinguished; it was only eclipsed. The light was still there, but it was covered. Peter and John were in the same spiritual condition, but soon all three of them would move out of the shadows and into the light.

2. Faith Dawning (John 20:3-10)

Verse 3 suggests that Peter started off first to run to the tomb, but verse 4 reports that John got there first. Perhaps John was a younger man in better physical condition, or perhaps John was just a better runner. It is tempting to "spiritualize" this footrace and relate it to Isaiah 40:31 and Hebrews 12:1-2. When a believer is out of fellowship with the Lord, it is difficult to run the race of faith. However, both men deserve credit for having the courage to run into enemy territory, not knowing what lay before them. The whole thing could have been a clever trap to catch the disciples.

When John arrived at the tomb, he cautiously remained outside and looked in. Perhaps he wanted Peter to be with him when he went into the burial chamber. What did John see? The graveclothes lying on the stone shelf without any evidence of violence or crime. *But the graveclothes were empty!* They lay there like an empty cocoon, still retaining the shape of Jesus' body.

Peter arrived and impulsively went into the tomb, just as we would expect him to do. He also saw the linen clothes lying there empty and the cloth for the head carefully rolled and lying by itself. Grave robbers do not carefully unwrap the corpse and then leave the graveclothes neatly behind. In fact, with the presence of the spices in the folds of the clothes, it would be almost impossible to unwrap a corpse without damaging the wrappings. The only way those linen clothes could be left in that condition would be if Jesus *passed through them* as He arose from the dead.

John then entered the tomb and looked at the evidence. "He saw, and believed."

When John wrote this account, he used three different Greek words for *seeing*. In verse 5, the verb simply means "to glance in, to look in." In verse 6, the word means "to look carefully, to observe." The word "saw" in verse 8 means "to perceive with intelligent comprehension." Their resurrection faith was now dawning!

It seems incredible that the followers of Jesus did not expect Him to come out of the tomb alive. After all, He had told them many times that He would be raised from the dead. Early in His ministry He had said, "Destroy this temple, and in three days I will raise it up" (2:19). After His resurrection, the disciples remembered that He had said this (2:22); however, His enemies remembered it too (Matt. 27:40, 63-64).

He compared Himself to Jonah (Matt. 12:40), and on two occasions clearly announced His resurrection after three days (Matt. 16:21; 20:19). On Thursday of His last week of ministry He again promised to be raised up and meet them in Galilee (Matt. 26:32, and see Luke 24:6-7).

What kind of faith did Peter and John have at that stage in their spiritual experience? They had faith based on evidence. They could see the graveclothes; they knew that the body of Jesus was not there. However, as good as evidence is to convince the mind, it can never change the life. Those of us who live centuries later cannot examine the evidence, for the material evidence (the tomb, the graveclothes) is no longer there for us to inspect. But we have the record in the Word of

God (John 20:9) and that record is true (19:35; 21:24). In fact, it is faith *in the Word* that the Lord really wanted to cultivate in His disciples (see 2:22; 12:16; 14:26). Peter made it clear that the Word of God should be the basis for our faith, not personal experiences (1 Peter 1:12-21).

The disciples had only the Old Testament Scriptures, so that is what is referred to in John 20:9. The early church used the Old Testament to prove to both Jews and Gentiles that Jesus is the Christ, that He died for sinners, and that He arose again (Acts 9:22; 13:16ff; 17:1-4; etc.). The Gospel includes "and that He arose again the third day according to the Scriptures" (1 Cor. 15:4). What Scriptures did Paul and John have in mind?

Paul saw the Resurrection in Psalm 2:7 (Acts 13:33). Peter saw it in Psalm 16:8-11 (Acts 2:23-36 and note 13:35). Peter also referred to Psalm 110:1 (Acts 2:34-35). The statement "he shall prolong his days" in Isaiah 53:10 is also interpreted as a prediction of Christ's resurrection. Jesus Himself used the Prophet Jonah to illustrate His own death, burial, and resurrection (Matt. 12:38-40); and this would include the "three days" part of the message. Paul saw in the Feast of Firstfruits a picture of the Resurrection (Lev. 23:9-14; 1 Cor. 15:20-23), and again, this would include "the third day." Some students see the Resurrection and "the third day" in Hosea 6:2.

After His resurrection, our Lord did not reveal Himself to everyone, but only to selected witnesses who would share the good news with others (Acts 10:39-43). This witness is now found in Scripture, the New Testament; and both the Old Testament and the New Testament agree in their witness. The Law, the psalms, the prophets, and the apostles together bear witness that Jesus Christ is alive!

Peter and John saw the evidence and believed. Later, the Holy Spirit confirmed their faith through the Old Testament Scriptures. That evening, they would meet the Master personally! Faith that was eclipsed has now started to dawn, and the light will get brighter.

3. Faith Shining (John 20:11-18)

When I think of Mary Magdalene lingering alone in the garden, I recall Proverbs 8:17—"I love them that love me; and those that seek me early shall find me." Mary loved her Lord and came early to the garden to express that love. Peter and John had gone home by the time Mary got back to the tomb, so they did not convey to her what conclusion they had reached from the evidence they had examined. Mary still thought that Jesus was dead. Another verse comes to mind—Psalm 30:5, "Weeping may endure for a night, but joy cometh in the morning."

Mary's weeping was the loud lamentation so characteristic of Jewish people when they express their sorrow (John 11:31, 33). There is certainly nothing wrong with sincere sorrow, because God made us to shed tears; and weeping is good therapy for broken hearts. The sorrow of the Christian, however, must be different from the hopeless sorrow of the world (1 Thes. 4:13-18), because we have been born again "unto a living hope by the resurrection of Jesus Christ from the dead" (1 Peter 1:3, NASB). We weep—not because our believing loved ones have gone to heaven—but because they have left us and we miss them.

When Mary looked into the sepulcher, she saw two men in white. Their position at either end of the shelf where the body had been lying makes us think of the cherubim on the mercy seat (Ex. 25:17-19). It is as though God is saying, "There is now a new mercy seat! My Son has paid the price for sin, and the way is open into the presence of God!" Mary apparently was not disturbed at seeing these men, and there is no evidence that she knew they were angels. The brief conversation neither dried her tears nor quieted her mind. She was determined to find the body of Jesus.

Why did Mary turn back and not continue her conversation with the two strangers? Did she hear a sound behind her? Or did the angels stand and recognize the presence of their Lord? Perhaps both of these speculations are true or neither is true. She was certain that the Lord's body was not in the tomb, so why linger there any longer?

Why did she not recognize the One for whom she was so earnestly searching? Jesus may have deliberately concealed Himself from her, as He would later do when He walked with the Emmaus disciples (Luke 24:13-32). It was still early and perhaps dark in that part of the garden. Her eyes were probably blinded by her tears as well.

Jesus asked her the same question that the angels had asked, "Why are you weeping?" How tragic that she was weeping when she could have been praising, had she realized that her Lord was alive! Then He added, "Whom are you seeking?" (He had asked the mob the same question in the garden—John 18:4.) It is encouraging to us to know that "Jesus knows all about our sorrows." The Saviour knew that Mary's heart was broken and that her mind was confused. He did not rebuke her; tenderly, He revealed Himself to her.

All He had to do was to speak her name, and Mary immediately recognized Him. His sheep hear [recognize] His voice and He calls them by name (10:3). Apparently Mary had turned away from Jesus, for when He spoke her name, she had to turn back to look at Him again. What a blessed surprise it was to see the face of her beloved Master!

All she could say was, "Rabboni—my Master, my Teacher." The title *Rabboni* is used in only one other place in the Gospels, Mark 10:51 (in the Greek text "Lord" is "Rabboni"). "Rabbi" and "Rabboni" were equivalent terms of respect. In later years, the Jews recognized three levels of teachers: rab (the lowest), rabbi, and rabboni (the highest).

Mary not only spoke to Him, but she grasped His feet and held on to Him. This was a natural gesture: now that she had found Him, she did not want to lose Him. She and the other believers still had a great deal to learn about His new state of glory; they still wanted to relate to Him as they had done during the years of His ministry before the cross.

Jesus permitted the other women to hold His feet (Matt. 28:9), and He did not forbid them. Why did He say to Mary, "Do not cling to Me"? One reason was that she would see Him again because He had not yet ascended to the Father. He remained on earth for forty days after His resurrection and often appeared to the believers to teach them spiritual truth (Acts 1:1-9). Mary had no need to panic; this was not her last and final meeting with the Lord.

A second reason is that she had a job to do—to go tell His brethren that He was alive and would ascend to the Father. "He is not ashamed to call them brethren" (Heb. 2:11). "I will declare thy name unto my brethren" (Ps. 22:22). He had called His own *servants* (13:16) and *friends* (15:15), but now He called them *brethren*. This meant that they shared His resurrection power and glory.

Some students feel that Jesus did return to the Father on that morning, and that was the ascension He was referring to; but no other New Testament passage corroborates this interpretation. To say that He was fulfilling the symbolism of the Day of Atonement and presenting the blood to the Father is, I think, stretching a type too far (Lev. 16). For that matter, *He had no blood to present;* He had presented that on the cross when He was made sin for us. In His resurrection glory, Jesus was "flesh and bones" (Luke 24:39), not "flesh and blood." The Resurrection itself was proof that the work of redemption had been completed ("raised because of our justification"—Rom. 4:24-25, NASB). What more could He do?

Our Lord never used the phrases "our Father" or "our God." His relationship to the Father was different from that of the disciples, and He was careful to make that distinction. We say "our Father" and "our God" because all believers belong to the same family and have an equal standing before God. He reminded Mary and the other believers that God was their

Father and that He would be with the Father in heaven after His ascension. In His Upper Room message, He had taught them that He would return to the Father so that the Spirit might come to them.

Although it was the same Jesus, only in a glorified body, it was not quite the same relationship. We must be careful not to relate to Christ "after the flesh" (1 Cor. 5:16), that is, relate to Him as though He were still in His state of humiliation. He is today the exalted Son of God in glory, and we must honor Him as such. The juvenile familiarity that some people display in public when they testify, pray, or sing only reveals that they have little understanding of Paul's words in 2 Corinthians 5:16. When John was with Jesus at the table, he leaned against His bosom (John 13:23); but when John saw Jesus on the Isle of Patmos, he fell at His feet as dead! (Rev. 1:17)

It would have been selfish and disobedient for Mary to have clung to Jesus and kept Him to herself. She arose and went to where the disciples were gathered and gave them the good news that she had seen Jesus alive. "I have seen the Lord!" (Note John 20:14, 18, 20, 25, 29.) Mark reports that these believers were mourning and weeping—and that they would not believe her! (Mark 16:9-11) Mary herself had been weeping, and Jesus had turned her sorrow into joy. If they had believed, their sorrow would also have turned to joy. Unbelief has a terribly deadening effect on a person. No wonder God warns us against "an evil heart of unbelief" (Heb. 3:12).

Mary not only shared the fact of His resurrection and that she had seen Him personally, but she also reported the words that He had spoken to her. Again, we see the importance of the Word of God. Mary could not transfer her experience over to them, but she could share the Word; and it is the Word that generates faith (Rom. 10:17). The living Christ shared His living Word (1 Peter 1:23-25).

It is good to have faith that is based on solid evidence, but the evidence should lead us to the Word, and the Word should lead us to the Saviour. It is one thing to accept a doctrine and defend it; it is something else to have a personal relationship to the living Lord. Peter and John believed that Jesus was alive, but it was not until that evening that they met the risen Christ in person along with the other disciples. (Jesus appeared to Peter sometime during the afternoon, 1 Cor. 15:5; Luke 24:34.) Evidence that does not lead to experience is nothing but dead dogma. The key is faith in the Word of God.

Dr. Robert W. Dale, one of Great Britain's leading Congregational pastors and theologians, was one day preparing an Easter sermon when a realization of the risen Lord struck him with new power.

"Christ is alive!" he said to himself. "Alive—alive—alive!" He paused, and then said, "Can that really be true? *Living* as really as I myself am?"

He got up from his desk and began to walk about the study, repeating, "Christ is living! Christ is living!"

Dr. Dale had known and believed this doctrine for years, but the reality of it overwhelmed him that day. From that time on, "the living Christ" was the theme of his preaching, and he had his congregation sing an Easter hymn every Sunday morning. "I want my people to get hold of the glorious fact that Christ is alive, and to rejoice over it; and Sunday, you know, is the day on which Christ left the dead."

Historical faith says, "Christ lives!"

Saving faith says, "Christ lives *in me!*"

Do you have saving faith?

11
The Power of His Resurrection
John 20:19-31

The news that Jesus was alive began to spread among His followers, at first with hesitation, but then with enthusiasm. Even His disciples did not believe the first reports, and Thomas demanded proof. But wherever people were confronted with the reality of His resurrection, their lives were transformed. In fact, that same transforming experience can be yours today. As you see in John 20:19-31 the changes that took place in the lives of people, ask yourself, "Have I personally met the risen Christ? Has He changed *my* life?"

1. From Fear to Courage (John 20:19-25)
Our Lord rested in the tomb on the Sabbath and arose from the dead on the first day of the week. Many people sincerely call Sunday "the Christian Sabbath," but Sunday is not the Sabbath Day. The seventh day of the week, the Sabbath, commemorates God's finished work of Creation (Gen. 2:1-3). The Lord's Day commemorates Christ's finished work of redemption, the "new creation." God the Father worked for six days and then rested. God the Son suffered on the cross for six hours, and then rested.

God gave the Sabbath to Israel as a special "sign" that they belonged to Him (Neh. 9:14; Ex. 20:8-11; 31:13-17). The nation was to use that day for physical rest and refreshment both for man and beast; but for Israel, it was not commanded as a special day of assembly and worship. Unfortunately, the scribes and Pharisees added all kinds of restrictions to the Sabbath observance until it became a day of bondage instead of a day of blessing. Jesus deliberately violated the Sabbath traditions, although He honored the Sabbath Day.

There were at least five resurrection appearances of our Lord on that first day of the week: to Mary Magdalene (John 20:11-18), the other women (Matt. 28:9-10), Peter (1 Cor. 15:5 and Luke 24:34), the two Emmaus disciples (Luke 24:13-32), and the disciples minus Thomas (John 20:19-25). The next Sunday, the disciples met again and Thomas was with them (John 20:26-31). It would appear that the believers from the very first met together on Sunday evening, which came to be called "the Lord's Day" (Rev. 1:10). It appears that the early church met on the first day of the week to worship the Lord and commemorate His death and resurrection (Acts 20:7; 1 Cor. 16:1-2).

The Sabbath was over when Jesus arose from the dead (Mark 16:1). He arose on the first day of the week (Matt. 28:1; Luke 24:1; John 20:1). The change from the seventh day to the first day was not effected by some church decree; it was brought about from the beginning by the faith and witness of the first believers. For centuries, the Jewish Sabbath had been associated with law: six days of work, and then you rest. But the Lord's Day, the first day of the week, is associated with grace: first there is faith in the living Christ, then there will be works.

There is no evidence in Scripture that God ever gave the original Sabbath command to the Gentiles, or that it was repeated for the church to obey. Nine of the Ten Commandments are repeated in the church epistles, but the Sabbath commandment is not repeated. However, Paul makes it clear that believers must not make "special days" a test of fellowship or spirituality (Rom. 14:5ff; Col. 2:16-23).

How did our Lord transform His disciples' fear into courage? For one thing, *He came to them.* We do not know where these ten frightened men met behind locked doors, but Jesus came to them and reassured them. In His resurrection body, He was able to enter the room without opening the doors! It was a solid body, for He asked them to touch Him—and He even ate some fish (Luke 24:41-43). But it was a different kind of body, one that was not limited by what we call "the laws of nature."

It is remarkable that these men were actually afraid. The women had reported to them that Jesus was alive, and the two Emmaus disciples had added their personal witness (Luke 24:33-35). It is likely that Jesus had appeared personally to Peter sometime that afternoon (1 Cor. 15:5; Luke 24:34; Mark 16:7), although Peter's *public* restoration would not take place until later (John 21). No wonder Jesus reproached them at that time "with their unbelief and hardness of heart" (Mark 16:14).

But His first word to them was the traditional greeting, "Shalom—peace!" He could have rebuked them for their unfaithfulness and cowardice the previous weekend, but He did not. "He hath not dealt with us after our sins; nor rewarded us according to our iniquities" (Ps. 103:10). The work of the cross is peace (Eph. 2:14-17; Rom. 5:1), and the message they would carry would be the Gospel of peace (Rom. 10:15). Man had declared war on God (Ps. 2; Acts 4:23-30), but God would declare "Peace!" to those who would believe.

Not only did Jesus come to them, but *He reassured them.* He showed them His wounded hands and side and gave them opportunity to discover that it was indeed their Master, and that He was not a phantom. (The Gospels do not record wounds in His feet, but Psalm 22:16 indicates that His feet were also nailed to the cross.)

But the wounds meant more than identification; they also were evidence that the price for salvation had been paid and man indeed could have "peace with God." The basis for all our peace is found in the Person and work of Jesus Christ. He died for us, He arose from the dead in victory, and now He lives for us. In our fears, we cannot lock Him out! He comes to us in grace and reassures us through His Word. "Faithful are the wounds of a friend" (Prov. 27:6).

When Jesus saw that the disciples' fear had not turned to joy, *He commissioned them:* "As My Father hath sent Me, even so send I you" (John 20:21). Keep in mind that the original disciples were not the only ones present; others, including the Emmaus disciples, were also in the room. This commission was not the "formal ordination" of a church order; rather, it was the dedication of His followers to the task of world evangelism. We are to take His place in this world (17:18). What a tremendous privilege and what a great responsibility! It is humbling to realize that Jesus loves us as the Father loves Him (15:9 and 17:26), and that we are in the Father just as He is (17:21-22). It is equally as humbling to realize that He has sent us into the world just as the Father sent Him. As He was about to ascend to heaven, He again reminded them of their commission to take the message to the whole world (Matt. 28:18-20).

It must have given the men great joy to realize that, in spite of their many failures, their Lord was entrusting them with His Word and His work. They had forsaken Him and fled, but now He was sending them out to represent Him. Peter had denied Him three times; and yet in a few days, Peter would preach the Word (and accuse the Jews of denying Him—Acts 3:13-14!) and thousands would be saved.

Jesus came to them and reassured them; but He also *enabled them* through the Holy Spirit. John 20:22 reminds us of Genesis 2:7 when God breathed life into the first man. In both

Hebrew and Greek, the word for "breath" also means "spirit." The breath of God in the first creation meant physical life, and the breath of Jesus Christ in the new creation meant spiritual life. The believers would receive the baptism of the Spirit at Pentecost and be empowered for ministry (Acts 1:4-5 and 2:1-4). Apart from the filling of the Spirit, they could not go forth to witness effectively. The Spirit had dwelt *with* them in the Person of Christ, but now the Spirit would be *in* them (John 14:17).

John 20:23 must not be interpreted to mean that Jesus gave to a select body of people the right to forgive sins and let people into heaven. Jesus had spoken similar words before (Matt. 16:19), but He was not setting aside the disciples (and their successors) as a "spiritual elite" to deal with the sins of the world. Remember, there were others in the room besides the disciples, and Thomas was missing!

A correct understanding of the Greek text helps us here. Some years ago, I corresponded with the eminent Greek scholar Dr. Julius R. Mantey (now deceased) about this verse, and he assured me that the correct translation both here and in Matthew 16:19 should be: "Whosoever sins you remit [forgive] shall have already been forgiven them, and whosoever sins you retain [do not forgive] shall have already not been forgiven them." In other words, the disciples did not provide forgiveness; they proclaimed forgiveness on the basis of the message of the Gospel. Another Greek scholar, Dr. Kenneth Wuest, translates it "they have been previously forgiven them."

As the early believers went forth into the world, they announced the good news of salvation. If sinners would repent and believe on Jesus Christ, their sins would be forgiven them! "Who can forgive sins but God only?" (Mark 2:7) All that the Christian can do is announce the message of forgiveness; God performs the miracle of forgiveness. If sinners will believe on Jesus Christ, we can authoritatively declare to them that their sins have been forgiven; but we are not the ones who provide the forgiveness.

By now, their fears had vanished. They were sure that the Lord was alive and that He was caring for them. They had both "peace with God" and the "peace of God" (Phil. 4:6-7). They had a high and holy commission and the power provided to accomplish it. And they had been given the great privilege of bearing the good news of forgiveness to the whole world. All they now had to do was tarry in Jerusalem until the Holy Spirit would be given.

2. From Unbelief to Confidence (John 20:26-28)

Why was Thomas not with the other disciples when they met on the evening of resurrection day? Was he so disappointed that he did not want to be with his friends? But when we are discouraged and defeated, we need our friends all the more! Solitude only feeds discouragement and helps it grow into self-pity, which is even worse.

Perhaps Thomas was afraid. But John 11:16 seems to indicate that he was basically a courageous man, willing to go to Judea and die with the Lord! John 14:5 reveals that Thomas was a spiritually minded man who wanted to know the truth and was not ashamed to ask questions. There seems to have been a "pessimistic" outlook in Thomas. We call him "Doubting Thomas," but Jesus did not rebuke him for his doubts. He rebuked him for unbelief: "Be not faithless, but believing." Doubt is often an intellectual problem: we want to believe, but the faith is overwhelmed by problems and questions. Unbelief is a moral problem; we simply will not believe.

What was it that Thomas would not believe? The reports of the other Christians that Jesus Christ was alive. The verb *said* in John 20:25 means that the disciples "kept saying to him" that they had seen the Lord Jesus Christ alive. No doubt the women and the Emmaus pilgrims also added their witness to this testimony. On the one hand, we admire Thomas for wanting *personal* experience; but on the other hand, we must fault him for laying down conditions for the Lord to meet.

Like most people in that day, he had two names: "Thomas" is Aramaic, "Didymus" is Greek, and they both mean "twin." Who was Thomas' twin? We do not know—but sometimes you and I feel as if we might be his twins! How often we have refused to believe and have insisted that God prove Himself to us!

Thomas is a good warning to all of us not to miss meeting with God's people on the Lord's Day (Heb. 10:22-25). Because Thomas was not there, he missed seeing Jesus Christ, hearing His words of peace, and receiving His commission and gift of spiritual life. He had to endure a week of fear and unbelief when he could have been experiencing joy and peace! Remember Thomas when you are tempted to stay home from church. You never know what special blessing you might miss!

But let's give him credit for showing up the next week. The other ten men had told Thomas that they had seen the Lord's hands and side (John 20:20), so Thomas made that the test. Thomas had been there when Jesus raised Lazarus, so why should he question our Lord's own resurrection? But, he still wanted proof; "seeing is believing."

Thomas' words help us to understand the difference between *doubt* and *unbelief.* Doubt says, "I cannot believe! There are too many problems!" Unbelief says, "I *will not* believe unless you give me the evidence I ask for!" In fact, in the Greek text, there is a double negative: "I positively will not believe!"

Jesus had heard Thomas' words; nobody had to report them to Him. So, the next Lord's Day, the Lord appeared in the room (again, the doors were locked) and dealt personally with Thomas and his unbelief. He still greeted them with "Shalom—peace!" Even Thomas' unbelief could not rob the other disciples of their peace and joy in the Lord.

How gracious our Lord is to stoop to our level of experience in order to lift us where we ought to be. The Lord granted

Gideon the "tests of faith" that he requested (Jud. 6:36-40), and He granted Thomas his request as well. There is no record that Thomas ever accepted the Lord's invitation. When the time came to prove his faith, Thomas needed no more proof!

Our Lord's words translate literally, "Stop becoming faithless but become a believer." Jesus saw a dangerous process at work in Thomas' heart, and He wanted to put a stop to it. The best commentary on this is Hebrews 3, where God warns against "an evil heart of unbelief" (v. 12).

It is not easy to understand the psychology of doubt and unbelief. Perhaps it is linked to personality traits; some people are more trustful than others. Perhaps Thomas was so depressed that he was ready to quit, so he "threw out a challenge" and never really expected Jesus to accept it. At any rate, Thomas was faced with his own words, and he had to make a decision.

John 20:29 indicates that Thomas' testimony did not come from his *touching* Jesus, but from his *seeing* Jesus. "My Lord and my God!" is the last of the testimonies that John records to the deity of Jesus Christ. The others are: John the Baptist (1:34); Nathanael (1:49); Jesus Himself (5:25 and 10:36); Peter (6:69); the healed blind man (9:35); Martha (11:27); and, of course, John himself (20:30-31).

It is an encouragement to us to know that the Lord had a personal interest in and concern for "Doubting Thomas." He wanted to strengthen his faith and include him in the blessings that lay in store for His followers. Thomas reminds us that unbelief robs us of blessings and opportunities. It may sound sophisticated and intellectual to question what Jesus did, but such questions are usually evidence of hard hearts, not of searching minds. Thomas represents the "scientific approach" to life—and it did not work! After all, when a skeptic says, "I will not believe unless—" he is already admitting that he does believe! He believes in the validity of the test or experiment that he has devised! If he can have faith in his own "scientific approach," why can he not have faith in what God has revealed?

We need to remind ourselves that everybody lives by faith. The difference is in the *object* of that faith. Christians put their faith in God and His Word, while unsaved people put their faith in themselves.

3. From Death to Life (John 20:29-31)

John could not end his book without bringing the resurrection miracle to his own readers. We must not look at Thomas and the other disciples and envy them, as though the power of Christ's resurrection could never be experienced in our lives today. *That was why John wrote this Gospel*—so that people in *every* age could know that Jesus is God and that faith in Him brings everlasting life.

It is not necessary to "see" Jesus Christ in order to believe. Yes, it was a blessing for the early Christians to see their Lord and know that He was alive; but that is not what saved them. They were saved, not by seeing, but by believing. The emphasis throughout the Gospel of John is on *believing*. There are nearly 100 references in this Gospel to believing on Jesus Christ.

You and I today cannot see Christ, nor can we see Him perform the miracles (signs) that John wrote about in this book. But the record is there, and that is all that we need. "So then faith cometh by hearing, and hearing by the word of God" (Rom. 10:17; and note 1 John 5:9-13). As you read John's record, you come face to face with Jesus Christ, how He lived, what He said, and what He did. All of the evidence points to the conclusion that He is indeed God come in the flesh, the Saviour of the world.

The signs that John selected and described in this book are proof of the deity of Christ. They are important. But sinners are not saved by believing in miracles; they are saved by believing on Jesus Christ. Many of the Jews in Jerusalem believed on

Jesus because of His miracles, but He did not believe in them (John 2:23-25)! Nicodemus believed in His miracles (3:2), but he was certainly not born again! Great crowds followed Him because of His miracles (6:2); but in the end, most of them left Him for good (6:66). Even the religious leaders who plotted His death believed that He did miracles, but this "faith" did not save them (11:47ff).

Faith in His miracles should lead to faith in His Word, and this leads to personal faith in Jesus as Saviour and Lord. Jesus Himself pointed out that faith in His works (miracles) was but *the first step* toward faith in the Word of God (5:36-40). The sinner must "hear" the Word if he is to be saved (5:24).

There was no need for John to decribe every miracle that our Lord performed; in fact, he supposed that a complete record could never be written (21:25). The life and ministry of Jesus Christ were simply too rich and full for any writer, even an inspired one, to give a complete record. But a complete record is not necessary. All of the basic facts are here for us to read and consider. There is sufficient truth for any sinner to believe and be saved!

The *subject* of John's Gospel is "Jesus is the Christ, the Son of God." He presented a threefold proof of this thesis: our Lord's works, our Lord's walk, and our Lord's words. In this Gospel, you see Jesus performing miracles; you watch Him living a perfect life in the midst of His enemies; and you hear Him speaking words that nobody else could speak.

Either Jesus was a madman, or He was deluded, or He was all that He claimed to be. While some of His enemies did call Him deranged and deluded, the majority of people who watched Him and listened to Him concluded that He was unique, unlike anyone else they had ever known. How could a madman or a deluded man accomplish what Jesus accomplished? *When people trusted Him, their lives were transformed!* That does not happen when you trust a madman or a deceiver.

He claimed to be God come in the flesh, the Son of God, the Saviour of the world. That is what He is!

John was not content simply to explain a subject. He was an evangelist who wanted to achieve an object. He wanted his readers to believe in Jesus Christ and be saved! He was not writing a biography to entertain or a history to enlighten. He was writing an evangel to change men's lives.

"Life" is one of John's key words; he uses it at least thirty-six times. Jesus offers sinners abundant life and eternal life; and the only way they can get it is through personal faith in Him.

If sinners need life, then the implication is that they are *dead*. "And you hath He quickened [made alive, resurrected] who were dead in trespasses and sins" (Eph. 2:1). Salvation is not resuscitation; it is resurrection (John 5:24). The lost sinner is not sick or weak; *he is dead.*

This life comes "through His name." What is His name? In John's Gospel, the emphasis is on His name "I AM." Jesus makes seven great "I AM" statements in this Gospel, offering the lost sinner all that he needs.

Eternal life is not "endless time," for even lost people are going to live forever in hell. "Eternal life" means *the very life of God experienced today*. It is a quality of life, not a quantity of time. It is the spiritual experience of "heaven on earth" today. The Christian does not have to die to have this eternal life; he possesses it in Christ today.

The ten disciples were changed from fear to courage, and Thomas was changed from unbelief to confidence. Now, John invites *you* to trust Jesus Christ and be changed from death to eternal life.

If you have already made this life-changing decision, give thanks to God for the precious gift of eternal life.

If you have never made this decision, *do so right now.*

"He that believeth on the Son hath everlasting life; and he that believeth not the Son shall not see life, but the wrath of God abideth on him" (3:36).

12

Transformed to Serve

John 21

The average reader would conclude that John completed his book with the dramatic testimony of Thomas (20:28-31), and the reader would wonder why John added another chapter. The main reason is the Apostle Peter, John's close associate in ministry (Acts 3:1). John did not want to end his Gospel without telling his readers that Peter was restored to his apostleship. Apart from the information in this chapter, we would wonder why Peter was so prominent in the first twelve chapters of the Book of Acts.

John had another purpose in mind: he wanted to refute the foolish rumor that had spread among the believers that John would live until the return of the Lord (21:23). John made it clear that our Lord's words had been greatly misunderstood.

I think John may have had another purpose in mind: he wanted to teach us how to relate to the risen Christ. During the forty days between His resurrection and ascension, our Lord appeared and disappeared at will, visiting with the disciples and preparing them for the coming of the Spirit and their future ministries (Acts 1:1-9). They never knew when He future ministries (Acts 1:1-9). They never knew when He would appear, so they had to stay alert! (The fact that He may return for His people *today* ought to keep us on our toes!) It was an important time for the disciples because they were about to take His place in the world and begin to carry the message to others.

I see in this chapter three pictures of the believer and a responsibility attached to each picture.

1. We Are Fishers of Men—Obey Him (John 21:1-8)

The Lord had instructed His disciples to meet Him in Galilee, which helps to explain why they were at the Sea of Galilee, or Sea of Tiberias (Matt. 26:32 and 28:7-10; Mark 16:7). But John did not explain why Peter decided to go fishing, and Bible students are not in agreement in their suggestions. Some claim that he was perfectly within his rights, that he needed to pay his bills and the best way to get money was to go fishing. Why sit around idle? Get busy!

Others believe that Peter had been called *from* that kind of life (Luke 5:1-11) and that it was wrong for him to return. Furthermore, when he went fishing, Peter took six other men with him! If he was wrong, they were wrong too; and it is a sad thing when a believer leads others astray.

By the way, it is interesting that at least seven of the twelve disciples were probably fishermen. Why did Jesus call so many fishermen to follow Him? For one thing, fishermen are courageous, and Jesus needs brave people to follow Him. They are also dedicated to one thing and cannot easily be distracted. Fishermen do not quit! (We are thinking, of course, of professional fishermen, not idle people on vacation!) They know how to take orders, and they know how to work together.

Whether Peter and his friends were right or wrong we cannot prove—although I personally think that they were wrong—but we do know this: their efforts were in vain. Had they forgotten the Lord's words, "For without Me, ye can do nothing"? (15:5) They toiled all night and caught nothing. Certainly, Peter must have remembered what happened two years before, when Jesus called him into full-time discipleship (Luke 5:1-11). On that occasion, Peter had fished all night and caught nothing, but Jesus had turned his failure into success.

Perhaps Peter's impulsiveness and self-confidence were revealing themselves again. He was sincere, and he worked hard, but there were no results. How like some believers in the service of the Lord! They sincerely believe that they are doing God's will, but their labors are in vain. They are serving without direction from the Lord, so they cannot expect blessing from the Lord.

After His resurrection, our Lord was sometimes not recognized (John 20:14; Luke 24:16); so it was that His disciples did not recognize Him when, at dawning, He appeared on the shore. His question expected a negative reply: "You have not caught anything to eat, have you?" Their reply was brief and perhaps a bit embarrassed: "No."

It was time for Jesus to take over the situation, just as He did when He called Peter into discipleship. He told them where to cast the net; they obeyed, and they caught 153 fish! The difference between success and failure was the width of the ship! We are never far from success when we permit Jesus to give the orders, and we are usually closer to success than we realize.

It was John who first realized that the stranger on the shore was their own Lord and Master. It was John who leaned on the Lord's breast at the table (13:23) and who stood by the cross when his Lord suffered and died (19:26). It is love that recognizes the Lord and shares that good news with others: "It is the Lord!"

With characteristic impulsiveness, Peter quickly put on his outer garment ("naked" simply means "stripped for work") and dove into the water! He wanted to get to Jesus! This is in contrast to Luke 5:8 where Peter told the Lord to depart from him. The other six men followed in the boat, bringing the net full of fish. In the experience recorded in Luke 5, the nets began to break; but in this experience, the net held fast.

Perhaps we can see in these two "fishing miracles" an illustration of how the Lord helps His people fish for lost souls. All of our efforts are useless apart from His direction and blessing. During this present age, we do not know how many fish we have caught, and it often appears that the nets are breaking! But at the end of the age, when we see the Lord, not one fish will be lost and we will discover how many there are.

Jesus called the disciples and us to be "fishers of men." This phrase was not invented by Jesus; it had been used for years by Greek and Roman teachers. To be a "fisher of men" in that day meant to seek to persuade men and "catch" them with the truth. A fisherman catches living fish, but when he gets them, they die. A Christian evangelist seeks to catch "dead fish" (dead in their sins), and when he or she "catches" them, they are made alive in Christ!

Now we can understand why Jesus had so many fishermen in the disciple band. Fishermen know how to work. They have courage and faith to go out "into the deep." They have much patience and persistence, and they will not quit. They know how to cooperate with one another, and they are skilled in using the equipment and the boat. What examples for us to follow as we seek to "catch fish" for Jesus Christ!

We are indeed "fishers of men," and there are "fish" all around us. If we obey His directions, we will catch the fish.

2. We Are Shepherds—Love Him (John 21:9-19)

Jesus met His disciples on the beach where He had already prepared breakfast for them. This entire scene must have stirred Peter's memory and touched his conscience. Surely he was recalling that first catch of fish (Luke 5:1-11) and perhaps even the feeding of the 5,000 with bread and fish (John 6). It was at the close of the latter event that Peter had given his clear-cut witness of faith in Jesus Christ (John 6:66-71). The "fire of coals" would certainly remind him of the fire at which he denied the Lord (18:18). It is good for us to remember the past; we may have something to confess.

Three "invitations" stand out in John's Gospel: "Come and see" (1:39); "Come and drink" (7:37); and "Come and dine" (21:12). How loving of Jesus to feed Peter before He dealt with his spiritual needs. He gave Peter opportunity to dry off, get warm, satisfy his hunger, and enjoy personal fellowship. This is a good example for us to follow as we care for God's people. Certainly the spiritual is more important than the physical, but caring for the physical can prepare the way for spiritual ministry. Our Lord does not so emphasize "the soul" that He neglects the body.

Peter and his Lord had already met privately and no doubt taken care of Peter's sins (Luke 24:34; 1 Cor. 15:5), but since Peter had denied the Lord *publicly,* it was important that there be a public restoration. Sin should be dealt with only to the extent that it is known. Private sins should be confessed in private, public sins in public. Since Peter had denied his Lord three times, Jesus asked him three personal questions. He also encouraged him by giving a threefold commission that restored Peter to his ministry.

The key issue is Peter's love for the Lord Jesus, and that should be a key matter with us today. But what did the Lord mean by "more than these"? Was He asking, "Do you love Me more than you love these other men?" Not likely, because this had never been a problem among the disciples. They all loved the Lord Jesus supremely, even though they did not always obey Him completely. Perhaps Jesus meant, "Do you love Me more than you love these boats and nets and fish?" Again, this is not likely, for there is no evidence that Peter ever desired to go back permanently into the fishing business. Fishing did not seem to compete with the Saviour's love.

The question probably meant, "Do you love Me—as you

claimed—more than these other disciples love Me?" Peter had boasted of his love for Christ and had even contrasted it with that of the other men. "I will lay down my life for Thy sake!" (John 13:37) "Though all men shall be offended because of Thee, yet will I never be offended!" (Matt. 26:33) There is more than a hint in these boastful statements that Peter believed that he loved the Lord more than did the other disciples.

Many commentaries point out that, in this conversation, two different words are used for "love." In His questions in John 21:15-16, our Lord used *agape*, which is the Greek word for the highest kind of love, sacrificing love, divine love. Peter always used *phileo*, which is the love of friend for friend, fondness for another. In v. 17, Jesus and Peter both used *phileo*.

However, it is doubtful that we should make too much of an issue over this, because the two words are often used interchangeably in the Gospel of John. In John 3:16, God's love for man is *agape* love; but in John 16:27, it is *phileo* love. The Father's love for His Son is *agape* love in 3:35 but *phileo* love in 5:20. Christians are supposed to love one another. In John 13:34, this love is *agape* love; but in 15:19, it is *phileo* love. It would appear that John used these two words as synonyms, whatever fine distinctions there might have been between them.

Before we judge Peter too severely, two other matters should be considered. When answering the first two questions, Peter did affirm his *agape* love when he said, "Yes, Lord!" The fact that Peter himself used *phileo* did not negate his wholehearted assent to the Lord's use of *agape*. Second, Peter and Jesus undoubtedly spoke in Aramaic, even though the Holy Spirit recorded the conversation in common Greek. It might be unwise for us to press the Greek too far in this case.

In spite of his faults and failures, Peter did indeed love the Lord, and he was not ashamed to admit it. The other men were certainly listening "over Peter's shoulder" and benefiting from the conversation, for they too had failed the Lord after boasting of their devotion. Peter had already confessed his sin and been forgiven. Now he was being restored to apostleship and leadership.

The image, however, changes from that of the fisherman to that of the shepherd. Peter was to minister both as an evangelist (catching the fish) and a pastor (shepherding the flock). It is unfortunate when we divorce these two because they should go together. Pastors ought to evangelize (2 Tim. 4:5) and then shepherd the people they have won so that they mature in the Lord.

Jesus gave three admonitions to Peter: "Feed My lambs," "Shepherd My sheep," and "Feed My sheep." Both the lambs and the more mature sheep need feeding and leading, and that is the task of the spiritual shepherd. It is an awesome responsibility to be a shepherd of God's flock! (1 Peter 5:2) There are enemies that want to destroy the flock, and the shepherd must be alert and courageous (Acts 20:28-35). By nature, sheep are ignorant and defenseless, and they need the protection and guidance of the shepherd.

While it is true that the Holy Spirit equips people to serve as shepherds, and gives these people to churches (Eph. 4:11ff), it is also true that each individual Christian must help to care for the flock. Each of us has a gift or gifts from the Lord, and we should use what He has given us to help protect and perfect the flock. Sheep are prone to wander, and we must look after each other and encourage each other.

Jesus Christ is the Good Shepherd (John 10:11), the Great Shepherd (Heb. 13:20-21), and the Chief Shepherd (1 Peter 5:4). Pastors are "under-shepherds" who must obey Him as they minister to the flock. *The most important thing the pastor can do is to love Jesus Christ.* If he truly loves Jesus Christ, the pastor will also love His sheep and tenderly care for them. (The Greek word for "sheep" at the end of John 21:17 means "dear sheep." Our Lord's sheep are dear to Him and He wants His ministers to love them and care for them personally and lovingly. (See Ezekiel 34 for God's indictment of unfaithful shepherds, the leaders of Judah.) A pastor who loves the flock will serve it faithfully, no matter what the cost.

3. We Are Disciples—Follow Him (John 21:18-25)

Jesus had just spoken about Peter's life and ministry, and now He talks about Peter's death. This must have been a shock to Peter, to have the Lord discuss his death in such an open manner. No doubt Peter was rejoicing that he had been restored to fellowship and apostleship. Why bring up martyrdom?

The first time Jesus spoke about His own death, Peter had opposed it (Matt. 16:21ff). Peter had even used his sword in the garden in a futile attempt to protect his Lord. Yet Peter had boasted he would die for the Lord Jesus! But when the pressure was on, Peter failed miserably. (You and I probably would have done worse!) Anyone who yields himself to serve the Lord must honestly confront this matter of death. As I write these words, the people of the United States are deeply mourning the tragic deaths of seven astronauts who died in the explosion of *Challenger*. Anyone involved in that kind of work knows that there are risks involved and must face the possibility of death.

When a person has settled the matter of death, then he is ready to live and to serve! Our Lord's own death is a repeated theme in John's Gospel: He knew that His "hour" would come, and He was prepared to obey the Father's will. We as His followers must yield ourselves—just as He yielded Himself for us—and be "living sacrifices" (Rom. 12:1-2) who are "ready to be offered" (2 Tim. 4:6-8) if it is the will of God.

Earlier that morning, Peter had "girded himself" and hurried to shore to meet Jesus (John 21:7). The day would come when another would take charge of Peter—and kill him. (See 2 Peter 1:13-14.) Tradition tells us that Peter was indeed crucified, but that he asked to be crucified upside down, because he was not worthy to die exactly as his Master had died.

But Peter's death would not be a tragedy; it would glorify God! The death of Lazarus glorified God (11:4 and 40) and so did the death of Jesus (12:23ff). Paul's great concern was that he glorify God, whether by life or by death (Phil. 1:20-21). This should be our desire as well.

Our Lord's words "Follow Me!" must have brought new joy and love to Peter's heart. Literally, Jesus said, "Keep on following Me." Immediately, Peter began to follow Jesus, just as he had done before his great denial. However, for a moment *Peter took his eyes off the Lord Jesus,* a mistake he had made at least two other times. After that first great catch of fish, Peter took his eyes off his Lord and looked at *himself.* "Depart from me; for I am a sinful man, O Lord!" (Luke 5:8) When he was walking on the stormy sea with Jesus, Peter looked away from the Lord and began to look at the wind and waves; and immediately he began to sink (Matt. 14:30). It is dangerous to look at the circumstances instead of looking to the Lord.

Why did Peter look away from his Lord and start to look back? He heard somebody walking behind him. It was the Apostle John who was also following Jesus Christ. Peter did a foolish thing and asked Jesus, "What shall this man do?" In other words, "Lord, you just told me what will happen to me; now, what will happen to John?"

The Lord rebuked Peter and reminded him that his job was to follow, not to meddle into the lives of other believers. Beware when you get your eyes off the Lord and start to look at other Christians! "Looking unto Jesus" should be the aim and practice of every believer (Heb. 12:1-2). To be distracted by ourselves, our circumstances, or by other Christians, is to disobey the Lord and possibly get detoured out of the will of God. Keep your eyes of faith on Him and on Him alone.

This does not mean that we ignore others, because we do

have the responsibility of caring for one another (Phil. 2:1-4). Rather, it means that we must not permit our curiosity about others to distract us from following the Lord. God has His plan for us; He also has plans for our Christian friends and associates. How He works in their lives is His business. Our business is to follow Him as He leads us. (See Romans 14:1-13.)

I recall a critical time in my own ministry when I was disturbed because other ministers were apparently getting God's "blessing" in abundance while I seemed to be reaping a meager harvest. I must confess that I envied them and wished that God had given their gifts to me. But the Lord tenderly rebuked me with, "What is that to thee? Follow thou Me." It was just the message I needed, and I have tried to heed it ever since.

Jesus did not say that John would live until His return, but that is the way some of the misguided believers understood it. More problems are caused by confused saints than by lost sinners! Misinterpreting the Word of God only creates misunderstanding about God's people and God's plans for His people.

However, there is a somewhat enigmatic quality to what the Lord said about John. Jesus did not say that John would live until He returned, nor did He say that John would die before He returned. As it was, John lived the longest of all the disciples and did witness the Lord's return when he saw the visions that he recorded in the Book of Revelation.

As John came to the close of his book, he affirmed again the credibility of his witness. (Remember, *witness* is a key theme in the Gospel of John. The word is used forty-seven times.) John witnessed these events himself and wrote them for us as he was led by the Holy Spirit. He could have included so much more, but he wrote only what the Spirit told him to write.

The book ends with Peter and John together following Jesus, and He led them right into the Book of Acts! What an exciting thing it was to receive the power of the Spirit and to bear witness of Jesus Christ! Had they not trusted Him, been transformed by Him, and followed Him, they would have remained successful fishermen on the Sea of Galilee; and the world would never have heard of them.

Jesus Christ is transforming lives today. Wherever He finds a believer who is willing to yield to His will, listen to His Word, and follow His way, He begins to transform that believer and accomplish remarkable things in that life. He also begins to do wonderful things through that life.

Peter and John have been off the scene (except for their books) for centuries, but you and I are still here. We are taking His place and taking their place. What a responsibility! What a privilege!

We can succeed only as we permit Him to transform us.
BE TRANSFORMED!

Chapter One

The Sovereign Servant
(John 13:1-35)

1. Describe a time when you have had to say farewell to someone. How did you feel?

2. Read John 13:1-35, which begins Jesus' farewell to His disciples. How did what Jesus knew lead to what He did?

3. What is significant about Jesus washing His disciples' feet?

4. What does Peter's response to Jesus washing their feet reveal about Peter?

5. What did Jesus teach through this act?

6. What do the disciples' responses to Jesus' announcement about His betrayal tell about them?

7. How did Jesus prepare His disciples for His death?

8. How would Jesus' death glorify God?

9. In what ways does our loving one another demonstrate that we belong to Jesus?

10. What can you do this week to show your love for another?

Chapter Two

Heart Trouble
(John 13:36–14:31)

1. What are some things that trouble you?

2. Read John 13:36–14:31. What troubled the disciples? Why?

3. How did Jesus calm His troubled disciples?

4. How did Jesus make heaven real to the disciples?

5. What does it mean to know the Father?

6. What are God's conditions for answering prayer? Why?

7. What does this passage teach us about the Holy Spirit?

8. How can the Holy Spirit help us when we're troubled?

9. Why did Jesus emphasize the relationship between loving Him and obeying Him?

10. How will you be obedient this week?

Chapter Three

Relationships and Responsibilities
(John 15:1-17)

1. What does it take for someone to be your friend?

2. Read John 15:1-17. What is significant about Jesus' use of the vine and branches to teach about a believer's relationship with Him?

3. How does God prune us? Why?

4. How can we abide in Jesus in our daily lives?

5. What fruit does God want us to produce?

6. What does friendship with Jesus involve?

7. How did Jesus demonstrate His friendship with the disciples?

8. What privileges do we have as Jesus' friends?

9. When is it hard for you to abide in Jesus? Why?

10. What can you do this week to abide in Jesus?

Chapter Four

What in the World Is the Spirit Doing?
(John 15:18–16:16)

1. How does the world make it hard for us to be Christians?

2. Read John 15:18–16:16. What did Jesus mean by the term the world?

3. Why does the world hate Christians?

4. How does the Holy Spirit encourage us when the world hates and opposes us?

5. Why is having the Holy Spirit more important than having the physical Jesus with us?

6. Of what does the Holy Spirit convict the world? Why?

7. How does the Holy Spirit convict the world?

8. How does the Holy Spirit teach believers?

9. What is the standard against which we should evaluate current teachings and manifestations about the Holy Spirit?

10. How will you let the Holy Spirit guide you this week?

Chapter Five

Let There Be Joy!
(John 16:16-33)

1. Describe a situation in your life when sorrow or pain has turned into joy.

2. Read John 16:16-33. What was the cause of the disciples' sorrow?

3. How was the disciples' sorrow transformed into joy?

4. What does Jesus say about joy?

5. What effect does each stage of Jesus' prediction have on His disciples?

6. Why did the disciples respond as they did to this news?

7. In what way did Jesus suggest that He knew the disciples' weaknesses as well as their faith?

8. What was the source of Jesus' encouragement when the disciples left Him?

9. What does it mean for us to have His peace in the world?

10. How are joy, prayer, and overcoming the world related?

11. How can you cooperate with God to experience His joy more fully during painful circumstances?

Chapter Six

The Prayer of the Overcomer
(John 17)

1. How do people try to get recognition for themselves?

2. Read John 17. Whose recognition was Jesus concerned about? Why?

3. Why did Jesus begin this prayer by praying for Himself?

4. How would you describe Jesus' relationship with the Father?

5. What were Jesus' requests for His disciples?

6. Why are we secure in Christ?

7. How does God's Word enable us to overcome the world?

8. How does God sanctify us through His truth?

9. What did Jesus pray for those who were to come, including us?

10. How can believers demonstrate true unity?

11. How does this prayer, in John 17, suggest we can share in Jesus' overcoming of the world?

12. In what ways do you need to change your priorities to match Jesus'?

Chapter Seven

Guilt and Grace in the Garden
(John 18:1-27)

1. What are some of the symbols that give shape to our lives every day?

2. Read John 18:1-27. What is significant about the symbols that are connected with Jesus in this passage—the garden and the cup?

3. What does Judas' kiss symbolize?

4. Why did the Roman soldiers and the religious leaders fall down when Jesus identified Himself?

5. What is significant about the symbols connected with Peter?

6. Why did Peter fail in trying to defend Jesus?

7. What steps did Peter take that led to his denial of Jesus?

8. How do we take the same steps in our own lives?

9. What did the cock crowing signify?

10. What evidences of guilt and grace do you find in this passage?

11. What can you do to help ensure that you won't deny Jesus this week?

Chapter Eight

"Suffered Under Pontius Pilate"

(John 18:28–19:16)

1. When are you tempted to do what will work instead of what is right? Why?

2. Read John 18:28–19:16. What did Pilate learn about Jesus from his conversation with the Jews?

3. What proof did the religious leaders have for their accusations against Jesus?

4. What do you learn about Pilate from the questions he asked Jesus?

5. Why did Jesus give the puzzling answers he gave?

6. How did Pilate try to do what would work instead of what he knew was right?

7. What do you learn about Jesus' humanity and deity from this passage?

8. Why do you think Jesus was silent during most of the second interview with Pilate?

9. On what did Pilate base his final decision about Jesus?

10. Why did God involve the Roman government in this situation?

11. What do you learn from Jesus' behavior before Pilate that helps us in our dealings with a hostile world?

Chapter Nine

"Even the Death of the Cross"
(John 19:17-42)

1. What sacrifices have other people made for you?

2. Read about Jesus' sacrifice for us in John 19:17-42. What do you know about crucifixion that sheds light on the way He died?

3. What is the significance of the inscription, in three languages, above the cross?

4. What did Pilate communicate with this inscription in spite of his motive?

5. What is significant about the women who were at the crucifixion?

6. What do you learn about Jesus from His actions on the cross?

7. Why did John use emphatic language to describe the blood and water flowing from Jesus' side?

8. Why did John write verse 35?

9. What is important about the fact that Jesus was buried?

10. What do you know about the two men who buried Jesus?

11. What does the pattern of prophecy and fulfillment suggest about God and His relation to history?

12. How can these truths help you live for God this week?

Chapter Ten

The Dawning of a New Day
(John 20:1-18)

1. When have you gone through a dark time that had a happy ending?

2. Read about the happy ending to Jesus' death in John 20:1-18. How do people try to explain away Jesus' resurrection?

3. What evidences are there in this passage that Jesus did indeed die and rise again?

4. How would you characterize Peter and John's faith at this time?

5. What do you learn about Mary from her experiences at the empty tomb and her encounter with the risen Christ?

6. Why were women the first witnesses of the resurrected Lord?

7. Why didn't Jesus appear in a more public way after His resurrection, such as to the Jewish leaders or to Pilate?

8. What role does evidence play in our conviction that Jesus is risen?

9. What transformations occurred in this passage?

10. How has the risen Lord transformed your life?

Chapter Eleven

The Power of His Resurrection
(John 20:19-31)

1. Describe a time when you have been afraid.

2. Read John 20:19-31. How did Jesus transform the disciples' fear to courage?

3. How does verse 22 parallel to other manifestations of the Holy Spirit in Scripture?

4. How are believers part of Jesus' divine prerogative for forgiving sins?

6. What was the nature of Thomas' doubt or unbelief?

7. What was Jesus' attitude toward Thomas?

8. How did Jesus approach Thomas? What was the result?

9. Why did John write this book?

10. What do you learn about believing from the last few verses?

11. What kind of life does faith lead to?

12. In what area do you need to let Jesus transform your fear or doubt into faith?

Chapter Twelve

Transformed to Serve
(John 21)

1. If you were going to paint a picture of a believer, what would it look like?

2. Read John 21 where John paints three pictures of believers. How did Peter's going fishing again fit his personality?

3. Why didn't the disciples recognize Jesus on the beach?

4. What did the disciples learn about obedience from this incident?

5. What is significant about Jesus sharing a meal with His disciples?

6. What do we learn from the second picture of believers in verses 9-19?

7. Why did Jesus compare His followers with sheep?

8. How does the command to "feed my sheep" contrast and compare with Jesus' previous command to be "fishers of men"?

9. Why did Jesus raise the matter of Peter's death at this point?

10. What's wrong with Peter's question about John in verse 21?

11. What is entailed in following Jesus as a disciple?

12. How can you be a disciple of Jesus this week?